Diplomacy and War at NATO

Diplomacy and War at NATO

*The Secretary General and
Military Action after the Cold War*

Ryan C. Hendrickson

*University of Missouri Press
Columbia and London*

Copyright © 2006 by
The Curators of the University of Missouri
University of Missouri Press, Columbia, Missouri 65201
Printed and bound in the United States of America
All rights reserved
5 4 3 2 1   10 09 08 07 06

Library of Congress Cataloging-in-Publication Data

Hendrickson, Ryan C., 1969–
    Diplomacy and war at NATO : the secretary general and military action
after the Cold War / Ryan C. Hendrickson.
        p. cm.
    Summary: "Examines the first four post–Cold War secretaries general—
Manfred Wörner, Willy Claes, Javier Solana, and George Robertson. Drawing
on interviews with former NATO ambassadors, alliance military leaders, and
senior NATO officials, Hendrickson demonstrates that the secretary general is
often the central diplomat in generating cooperation within NATO"—
Provided by publisher.
    Includes bibliographical references and index.
    ISBN-13: 978-0-8262-1664-9 (hard cover : alk. paper)
    ISBN-10: 0-8262-1664-1 (hard cover : alk. paper)
    ISBN-13: 978-0-8262-1635-9 (pbk. : alk. paper)
    ISBN-10: 0-8262-1635-8 (pbk. : alk. paper)
    1. North Atlantic Treaty Organization. 2. World politics—1989–
3. Military history, Modern—20th century. 4. Military history, Modern—21st
century. I. Title.
    UA646.3.H358 2006
    355'.031091821—dc22
                                                                                                    2005031554

⊗ ™ This paper meets the requirements of the
American National Standard for Permanence of Paper
for Printed Library Materials, Z39.48, 1984.

Designer: Foley Design
Typesetter: Crane Composition, Inc.
Printer and binder: The Maple-Vail Book Manufacturing Group
Typefaces: Bernhard and Palatino

Contents

Acknowledgments

Before thanking the many individuals who were instrumental in helping me complete this book, I must first note that three chapters of this book were published previously, although in different form. Much of Chapter 2 appeared as "Leadership at NATO: Secretary Manfred Woerner and the Crisis in Bosnia," in the *Journal of Strategic Studies* 27, no. 3 (2004): 508–27. Part of Chapter 3 was published as "NATO's Secretary General and the Use of Force: Willy Claes and the Air Strikes in Bosnia," in *Armed Forces and Society* 31, no. 1 (2004): 95–118. Some of the research presented in Chapter 4 also appeared as "NATO's Secretary General Javier Solana and the Kosovo Crisis," in the *Journal of International Relations and Development* 5, no. 3 (2002): 240–57, and is reproduced with permission granted by the Faculty of Social Sciences at the University of Ljubljana, Centre of International Relations.

Many previous and current U.S. and international government officials associated with NATO agreed to be interviewed for this book. Some of these officials include John Anderson, Reginald Bartholomew, James K. Bartleman, Robin Beard, Stanton Burnett, R. Nicholas Burns, Daniel Christman, Robert George, Robert Hunter, Thorstein Ingolfsson, George Joulwan, Karel Kovanda, Anthony Lake, Leif Mevik, Thomas Montgomery, Jerzy Nowak, Joseph Ralston, Jamie Shea, Dominique Struye de Swieland, and Lambert Willem Veenendaal. They were all kind to grant me interviews and share their time with me. Many other NATO officials and United

States Department of Defense officials were interviewed who asked not to be identified. For those who cannot be cited—I thank you, too.

Many academic colleagues critiqued my research, pointed me in the right direction, or simply encouraged my work on this book through different forms of support. Some of these individuals include Rick Atkinson, Bob Augustine, Chris Bennett, Craig Cobane, Paul Diehl, Patrick James, Lawrence Kaplan, Kent Kille, Andrew McNitt, Robert Owen, Nicholas Sherwin, Patricia Shields, and Richard Wandling. Among my many supportive colleagues, Mike Schechter was especially helpful in encouraging me to think of this project in its early stages as an eventual book manuscript. Jon Clausen merits special thanks for his willingness to share in my enthusiasm for the information gathered in my interviews with various NATO officials, especially regarding my findings on Willy Claes and NATO's 1995 air strikes in Bosnia.

I benefited tremendously from the external reviews of the book, and am especially grateful to Sean Kay, who provided useful critiques of the entire manuscript. He was also instrumental in steering me in the right direction in Brussels. Although Dave Forsythe was not directly involved in this research, I continue to greatly appreciate and benefit from his research mentoring while I was at the University of Nebraska–Lincoln.

Finally, above all, it is my family that deserves the most thanks. My parents, Jerry and Mary Hendrickson, were always enthusiastic and optimistic supporters of this book. My wife, Tece, deserves thanks for essentially everything—but mostly for her patience and encouragement in all aspects of this project. Marguerite Mary, Frances, and Ryan Warren also need to be mentioned and thanked in this book. Marguerite and Frances's phone "conversation" with Stanton Burnett, who was my final interview for this book, made for one of my most memorable research experiences, and will certainly go down as a classic in our family.

Diplomacy and War at NATO

Introduction

In the early 1990s, with the collapse of the Soviet Union, the North Atlantic Treaty Organization (NATO) faced fundamental questions regarding its purpose and mission. By the end of the decade, however, NATO had evolved into a fundamentally different security organization, and had arguably become the centerpiece for American foreign policy during the Clinton administration. For the first time in its history, NATO engaged in military air strikes: first on the Bosnian Serbs in 1994 and 1995, and then in Kosovo and the wider Yugoslavia in 1999. The alliance also expanded its membership across Central and Eastern Europe, and it undertook new missions in peacekeeping, peace enforcement, and crisis prevention. In many respects, NATO became the world's most important international organization, as it wielded its military power across the Balkans and attempted to stabilize and transform the new European democracies. NATO assumed a dramatically new and heightened role in international security during the 1990s, one that was vastly different from its traditional Cold War function of containing communism.[1]

Some prominent observers of international politics predicted that NATO would collapse in the Soviet Union's absence. Traditional "realist" theorists of international relations argued that alliances need enemies to hold them together. Without an adversary, such

1. See Richard L. Kugler, *Commitment to Purpose: How Alliance Partnership Won the Cold War* (Washington, DC: RAND, 1993).

1

military organizations no longer serve their members' national interests, and so, they believed, this change would eventually lead to NATO's collapse.[2] Counter to these predictions, however, events in the 1990s demonstrated that NATO adapted to the new security milieu as it evolved and undertook new military and diplomatic roles across Europe. Although the NATO allies experienced a divisive and open debate over the organization's role with the Iraq crisis in 2003, NATO's transformation clearly continues, with its peacekeeping operation in Afghanistan, its formal induction of seven new members in 2004, and its ongoing peacekeeping efforts across the Balkans.

Given NATO's historic evolution in the post–Cold War era, a considerable amount of scholarly attention has been devoted to understanding its transformation. Some analysts have focused on the new strategic/conceptual changes NATO adopted initially at its London and Rome Summits in 1990 and 1991, when the alliance agreed to new security missions across Europe. Other research on the alliance's evolution examines its military and peacekeeping activities in Bosnia and Kosovo, and includes military assessments of the bombing operations in the Balkans. Still other analysts examine the alliance's decision to expand its membership in two rounds: first at the Madrid Summit in 1997, and later at the Prague Summit in 2002. Much of this research focuses on the political explanations for expansion, as well as on examinations of the costs and benefits of NATO's new member states.[3]

Within this body of literature and in the wider literature on American foreign policy, however, no sustained and comparative analysis of NATO's political leader, the secretary general, exists. The secretary general, who is traditionally a European diplomat, attempts to promote transatlantic consensus among the allies at NATO's political headquarters in Brussels, Belgium. In doing so, the secretary general assumes a very public role for NATO, serving as its principal spokesperson and advocate for unity. When it comes

2. John J. Mearsheimer, "Back to the Future: Instability in Europe after the Cold War," *International Security* 15, no. 1 (1990): 5–57; Kenneth N. Waltz, "The Emerging Structure of International Politics," *International Security* 18, no. 2 (1993): 44–79.

3. See the Bibliographic Essay for sources on NATO's post–Cold War evolution, its military operations in Bosnia and Kosovo, and its expansion.

to specific research on NATO's secretaries general, either during the Cold War or after it, a significant analytical void exists. If analysts mention the secretary general at all, which occurs infrequently at best, he is often described as a leader who operated under serious (and in some cases, profound) political and organizational constraints.[4]

One exception to the Cold War scholarship on NATO's secretary general is Robert S. Jordan's *Political Leadership in NATO*, which chronicles the Cold War secretaries general from 1952 to 1971.[5] While Jordan notes that the secretaries general frequently had serious political constraints placed upon them, he maintains that all were nonetheless skilled diplomats who provided independent influence on various organizational aspects of NATO. While he does not credit them with being central policy makers and transformative individuals during the alliance's major decision-making procedures or its crises, he still regards them as talented diplomats who were often able to enhance alliance cooperation. Jordan's book, however, is exceptional in that it is the only research devoted solely to NATO's secretaries general. Otherwise, almost no research exists on the Cold War secretaries general, and this is also true of the post–Cold War secretaries general.

Given this absence of attention, one might reach the conclusion that the secretaries general were minor players in the alliance's post–Cold War transformation. Seemingly, other factors such as American leadership of the alliance, the international crises taking place in the Balkans that forced NATO to accept new missions, or natural organizational evolution may be better indicators for explaining how NATO remained relevant in the 1990s and into the next decade. Such a finding would generally square with the wider research on leaders of intergovernmental organizations (IGOs). While it has been demonstrated that the United Nations secretary general, the European Union Commission president, and the World

4. Several books and articles that discuss, in part, the difficulties of the secretaries general in trying to independently make changes in NATO policy are listed in the Bibliographic Essay.
5. Robert S. Jordan with Michael W. Bloome, *Political Leadership in NATO: A Study in Multinational Diplomacy* (Boulder, CO: Westview Press, 1979). See also Robert S. Jordan, ed., *Generals in International Politics* (Lexington, KY: University Press of Kentucky, 1987).

Bank president, among other IGO leaders, can play an important role in shaping policy, much research on IGO leaders points to the institutional constraints of these offices. These constraints may include the member states' ongoing protection of their own political sovereignty, the absence of supportive international public opinion, or the inherent institutional leadership limits of these offices, among other factors.[6] Although this study does not disregard previously identified forces in explaining NATO's transformation, it indicates that NATO's secretary general has been an under-examined political influence in the alliance and, at times, a critical player in shaping NATO's post–Cold War evolution.

Using an analytical framework based on Michael G. Schechter's research on leaders of IGOs, this book examines the first four post–Cold War secretaries general and the roles they played in moving the alliance toward military action.[7] The findings suggest that Manfred Wörner, Willy Claes, Javier Solana, and Lord George Robertson differed in the kind of impact they had on the alliance, but nonetheless that they all were critical players in shaping how and when NATO used force. Exceptional diplomatic skills, creative uses of NATO's rules, different degrees of backing from NATO's major powers, and their relationships with the supreme allied commander, Europe (the SACEUR, NATO's foremost military official), permitted these secretaries general at times to personally affect NATO and its corresponding military actions. These findings provide new explanations for how NATO was able to transform itself in the Soviet Union's absence and, in certain instances, for specific military and political decisions made while the alliance was engaged in combat.

6. Kent J. Kille and Roger M. Scully, "Executive Heads and the Role of Intergovernmental Organizations: Expansionist Leadership in the United Nations and European Union," *Political Psychology* 24, no. 1 (2003): 175–98; Edward Newman, *The UN Secretary General from the Cold War to the New Era: Global Peace and Security Mandate?* (New York: St. Martin's Press, 1998); Benjamin Rivlin and Leon Gordenker, eds., *The Challenging Role of the UN Secretary General: Making "The Most Impossible Job in the World" Possible* (Westport, CT: Praeger, 1993).

7. The model is in Michael G. Schechter's "Leadership in International Organizations: Systemic, Organizational and Personality Factors," *Review of International Studies* 13, no. 3 (1987): 197–220.

By focusing on these four individuals, this book provides another analytical lens for understanding how NATO evolves and adds new historical explanations for NATO's use of force in Bosnia and Kosovo and for its decision to provide Article 4 security guarantees to Turkey in February 2003 before Operation Iraqi Freedom. Although a host of political factors are relevant for understanding NATO's transformation, this book maintains that the individuals who served as NATO's secretary general had substantial effects on NATO policy and were critical players in its post–Cold War evolution.

ORGANIZATION OF THE BOOK

Because so little research has been devoted to NATO's secretary general, the first chapter of this book provides a historical overview of the creation of this office in 1952 and offers short discussions of all the Cold War secretaries general. In all cases discussed, these leaders had significant influence on how the alliance conducted business and reached transatlantic unity. At the same time, however, the Cold War secretaries general exercised leadership in a very different political context from those who led after the Cold War, and none oversaw NATO when the organization used force. In this respect, their leadership tenures were unlike those of the four individuals examined in this book; their missions were fundamentally different from their post–Cold War successors' missions.

The book follows with comparative case studies of the first four post–Cold War secretaries general. Using interviews with key diplomats and NATO policy makers, each chapter centers on the role of the secretary general in use-of-force decisions, focusing on those occasions when military conduct was either contemplated or implemented. Admittedly, such an approach examines only one element of each individual's leadership. Yet the use of force was, arguably, NATO's most important action in its post–Cold War evolution. Certainly, other issues addressed at NATO are worthy of examination, but by focusing primarily on actual military decisions for the alliance, the research effort can be narrowed and focused, and the comparative value of each chapter increases. Each chapter also provides a brief historical background on the origins of the conflict under examination and includes a discussion of how each secretary general came to his position.

More specifically, Chapter 2 begins with an extended description of the analytical framework that is used to examine the influence of the secretaries general on use-of-force decisions for the alliance in the post–Cold War era, which includes a discussion of how these leaders exercised influence at the systemic level, at the organizational level, and vis-à-vis NATO's supreme allied commander. It follows with an examination of Secretary General Manfred Wörner's role in moving the alliance toward military action in Bosnia in 1993 and 1994. Although NATO fell far short of what Wörner personally sought for Bosnia, he nonetheless played a key role at the organizational level in shaping alliance policies on Bosnia.

Chapter 3 assesses Secretary General Willy Claes's influence in shaping alliance policies prior to and during Operation Deliberate Force, NATO's two-week bombing campaign against the Bosnian Serbs in 1995. Although Claes's leadership and legacy have been overshadowed by his involvement with a bribery scandal stemming from his earlier days in Belgian politics, the findings presented here suggest that Claes was quite important at the organizational level, as well as in his relationship with SACEUR George Joulwan, in shaping NATO's actions during its first sustained military campaign.

Chapter 4 turns to the instrumental role played by Javier Solana during Operation Allied Force, the seventy-eight-day bombing campaign in Yugoslavia in 1999. The research presented in this chapter suggests that Solana was critical in shaping NATO's political and military agenda at the systemic and organizational levels, and that he played a key role for the alliance working with SACEUR Wesley Clark during Operation Allied Force. Solana's diplomatic style was also considerably different from both of his predecessors', but his influence was extensive.

Chapter 5 follows with a study of Secretary General Lord George Robertson's efforts to promote transatlantic consensus on the issue of Iraq, culminating in NATO's decision to provide some military defensive measures to Turkey in 2003 under Article 4 of the North Atlantic Treaty. While Robertson's legacy will be fundamentally different from those of the previous three secretaries general, he was nonetheless a very influential leader, especially at the organizational level.

The concluding chapter summarizes the findings, offers a comparative assessment of effective diplomatic leadership in NATO, and provides policy recommendations for the improvement of transatlantic tensions surrounding the office of the secretary general. In sum, this book attempts to fill a major void in the academic literature on NATO's post–Cold War transformation, its organizational leadership, and its major military actions since the Soviet Union's collapse. The chapters that follow give examples and analyses of creative and skilled diplomats, which may provide some insight on how to build and improve upon a troubled transatlantic relationship.

1

NATO's Cold War Secretary General

Many analysts and political decision makers have viewed the North Atlantic Treaty Organization (NATO) as history's most successful military alliance. NATO is a security and political organization that, at its core, was intended to protect Western Europe from a Soviet military intervention during the Cold War. The movement to create NATO and eventually the office of the secretary general, however, did not occur in a political vacuum; it demanded a nexus of favorable domestic political conditions in the United States, as well as strong advocates in Europe for transatlantic cooperation.

NATO's CREATION

Although NATO's history stems from the Cold War's onset, the seeds of its origin were planted during the Second World War. During the war, it became especially clear to the United Kingdom that its short- and long-term interests were served through its military alliance with the United States. In 1943, in a speech at Harvard University, British prime minister Winston Churchill suggested that the American and British partnership had long-term political and military value and should be continued at the war's end. A 1944 classified British study also suggested that a collective security organization including the United States, the United Kingdom, and the rest of the European allies would be the best policy direction for the British after the war.[1] Although the United States later played a critical and determinative role in forming the alliance, much of the historical record indicates that the initial movement for a permanent transatlantic alliance was in the United Kingdom.

After the Second World War, with the United States' ascent to its leadership position in international affairs, the Roosevelt administration proved instrumental in creating the United Nations, as well as the Bretton Woods Institutions—the International Monetary Fund and the World Bank. NATO was not an immediate result of the war, but the newly perceived threat of the Soviet Union proved to be the most important catalyst for the initial American interest in an alliance. Having not fulfilled his promises from the Yalta Conference in 1945, Premier Joseph Stalin of the Soviet Union demonstrated little interest in democratizing and liberalizing Eastern Europe. In 1947, the Truman administration responded with a massive and historic foreign-assistance program to Europe, the Marshall Plan, in an effort to rebuild the capitalist Western European democracies and to strengthen Europe's existing democratic political leaders. In the same year, President Harry Truman announced that the United States would provide financial aid to Greece and Turkey, a plan that became known as the "Truman Doctrine," and this indicated that the United States would defend democracy against anti-democratic forces. Such policies and American leadership were welcomed by the European democracies, but Ernest Bevin, the British foreign minister, soon communicated to the United States that the Marshall Plan would not be enough to guarantee European democracy against the Soviet threat. Although Bevin was not necessarily suggesting the presence of American troops or a treaty, he was clearly seeking a greater political commitment from the United States to European security.[2]

In 1948, heightened Cold War threats produced new momentum for a transatlantic alliance. In February 1948, the democratic- and West-leaning Czechoslovakian foreign minister, Jan Masaryk, was murdered by either Soviet agents or their Czechoslovakian allies.

1. Sean Kay, *NATO and the Future of European Security* (Lanham, MD: Rowman and Littlefield, 1998), 13–14.

2. Lawrence S. Kaplan, *The United States and NATO: The Formative Years* (Lexington, KY: University Press of Kentucky, 1984), 51.

This event galvanized the American foreign-policy elite and provided additional momentum for an alliance with Europe.[3]

With American approval, Britain, France, and the Benelux states (Belgium, Luxembourg, and the Netherlands) created the Brussels Treaty on March 17, 1948. All the states agreed to come to each other's defense upon attack. At the same time, it was understood by all that this alliance was an inadequate security guarantee against the Soviet Union without American backing. Even the traditionally neutral Scandinavian states of Denmark, Iceland, and Norway, who were moving toward creating a Scandinavian Defense Union, agreed that American military support was now needed in a formal new alliance. Among the Scandinavians, Norway was the strongest advocate for American leadership in the proposed transatlantic alliance. Even Sweden, which did not become a member of NATO, quietly cooperated with the NATO allies.[4]

In secret conferences held in Washington in early 1948, representatives from the United States, Canada, and the United Kingdom met to produce the first draft documents for a formal military alliance. Diplomatic pressure also came from France, which, like the rest of Europe, was becoming increasingly alarmed at Soviet actions in Eastern Europe. More importantly, France had ongoing fears (if not paranoia) of a German military resurgence, and thus was advocating for the presence of American troops in continental Europe.[5] Thus, by 1948 a consensus existed among the major European democracies that an American-European military alliance was necessary to secure Europe.

Within the United States, one of the biggest political hurdles to overcome was potential opposition from the conservative Republican chairman of the Senate Foreign Relations Committee, Senator Arthur H. Vandenberg (R-MI). Although more than a quarter of a century had passed since the Republican-led rejection of President Woodrow Wilson's Treaty of Versailles and his desire for American membership in the League of Nations, the Truman administration's memory had not faded on the potential political power that an in-

3. Ibid., 61.

4. Ingermar Dörfer, *The Nordic Nations in the New Western Security Regime* (Washington, DC: Woodrow Wilson Center Press, 1997), 70–71.

5. Kaplan, *The United States and NATO*, 68; Kay, *NATO and the Future of European Security*, 20; Stanley R. Sloan, *NATO, the European Union, and the Atlantic Community* (Lanham, MD: Rowman and Littlefield, 2003), 17–18.

dividual senator could wield, just as Senator Henry Cabot Lodge (R-MA) had done in 1919, when he led the Senate against Wilson's internationalism. The Truman administration understood that strong sentiments still remained in the United States for avoiding "entangling alliances," which President George Washington had warned against in his farewell address to the nation. Some members of the Senate, including Vandenberg, were also concerned about a new military alliance and the need for compatibility with the principles provided in the United Nations Charter.

As the policy proposals in the Truman administration moved toward a transatlantic military agreement, Vandenberg was consulted extensively and included on key committees dealing with the creation of the alliance. This strategy yielded immense political dividends for the Truman administration, as Vandenberg eventually sponsored the "Vandenberg Resolution," which called for the United States to move toward a military alliance with Europe in response to the growing Soviet threat. The Senate passed the resolution on June 11, 1948, but with the understanding that the European governments would cooperate in sharing the financial and military burden of protecting themselves. Its passage was a revolutionary step for the Senate, given its historic role in preventing American membership in the League of Nations and the isolationist tendencies of a number of senior Republicans.[6]

In the summer of 1948, the Soviet Union also began its blockade of Berlin, Germany, which generated additional international momentum for a permanent military alliance. Backroom negotiations between the European powers and the United States, led by American John D. Hickerson, director of the U.S. State Department's Office of European Affairs, eventually led to the North Atlantic Treaty, passed on April 4, 1949.[7] NATO included twelve member countries at its inception. Much of the diplomatic negotiations prior to the treaty's acceptance focused on which countries would belong to NATO, with considerable debate over Italy's and especially Portugal's membership, given that Portugal was not a democracy at the time and had declared a policy of neutrality during the Second World War. The opposition to Portugal's membership was led by

6. See Kaplan, *The United States and NATO,* 77.
7. Ibid., 110; Kay, *NATO and the Future of European Security,* 20. The treaty is in the Appendix.

the Canadian government, which viewed NATO as both a military and a *political* organization, where values should be shared by all members. Given Portugal's geostrategic importance near the Mediterranean, though, and the quiet support it had given the allies during the Second World War, Canada soon dropped its opposition. With American support and Hickerson's diplomatic skills, the final initial membership included both Italy and Portugal, as well as Belgium, Canada, Denmark, France, Iceland, Luxembourg, the Netherlands, Norway, the United Kingdom, and the United States.[8]

The North Atlantic Treaty's cornerstone is Article 5, which states in part:

> The Parties agree that an armed attack against one or more of them in Europe or North America shall be considered an attack against them all and consequently they agree that, if such an attack occurs, each of them, in exercise of the right of individual or collective self-defence recognised by Article 51 of the Charter of the United Nations, will assist the Party or Parties so attacked by taking forthwith, individually and in concert with the other Parties, such action as it deems necessary, including the use of armed force, to restore and maintain the security of the North Atlantic area.[9]

In short, if any alliance member would be attacked, all agreed to come to its defense.[10] The North Atlantic Treaty was revolutionary and historic in that it "entangled" the United States formally in European affairs. For the Europeans, the treaty represented their

---

8. On the Italian and Portuguese membership issues, see Mark Smith, *NATO Enlargement during the Cold War: Strategy and System in the Western Alliance* (New York: Palgrave, 2000), 28–50; Robert H. Ferrell, "The Formation of the Alliance, 1948–1949," in *American Historians and the Atlantic Alliance*, ed. Lawrence S. Kaplan (Kent, OH: Kent State University Press, 1991), 22–24.

9. North Atlantic Treaty, Article 5. See Appendix.

10. Article 11 of the North Atlantic Treaty demands that the "constitutional processes" of each member state be respected prior to the use of force. In the United States, members of the Senate understood that they were not abdicating their congressional "war powers" to the president in consenting to the treaty. See Michael J. Glennon, "United States Mutual Security Treaties: The Commitment Myth," *Columbia Journal of Transnational Law*, 24, no. 3 (1986): 535; and Ryan C. Hendrickson, *The Clinton Wars: The Constitution, Congress and War Powers* (Nashville, TN: Vanderbilt University Press, 2002), 10–13.

military dependency upon the United States. Although a number of issues remained unresolved at the time, notably, how integrated American forces would be with their European counterparts, and how Germany fit into NATO's future, the treaty set the stage for a much different Cold War containment strategy, with a considerably heightened role for the United States in Europe.[11]

The Organization and the Office of Secretary General

Originally, NATO existed with little formal organization. The most specific reference to the structure of the organization was made in Article 9 of the treaty, which states, "The Parties hereby establish a Council, on which each of them shall be represented, to consider matters concerning the implementation of this Treaty. The Council shall be so organised as to be able to meet promptly at any time. The Council shall set up such subsidiary bodies as may be necessary; in particular it shall establish immediately a defence committee which shall recommend measures for the implementation of Articles 3 and 5."[12]

In its infancy, however, the North Atlantic Council (NAC) amounted to little more than biannual meetings of the foreign ministers of NATO's member countries with very little real organization or rules for the newly created alliance. In May 1950, at its London Summit, NATO created a Council of Deputies consisting of civilian leaders who worked on behalf of their respective foreign ministers to promote cooperation between two existing committees, the Defense Committee, made up of member states' defense ministers, and the Defense, Financial, and Economic Committee, which was led by the members' finance ministers. All committees were stationed in London. These developments, however, were soon seen as only partial solutions to the alliance's real organizational needs.[13]

The principal catalyst for NATO's organizational development was the beginning of the Korean War in June 1950. North Korean

---

11. Sloan, *NATO, the European Union, and the Atlantic Community*, 16–17.
12. North Atlantic Treaty, Article 9. See Appendix.
13. Robert S. Jordan with Michael W. Bloome, *Political Leadership in NATO: A Study in Multinational Diplomacy* (Boulder, CO: Westview Press, 1979), 8; Kay, *NATO and the Future of European Security*, 33.

military advances prompted the United States to call for improved military coordination of NATO, culminating in the December 19, 1950, appointment of General Dwight Eisenhower to serve as NATO's first supreme allied commander, Europe (SACEUR). Symbolically, Eisenhower's appointment indicated the Truman administration's heightened commitment to the alliance, given Eisenhower's international reputation and the historic role he had played in the Second World War. On his appointment as SACEUR, it has been noted of Eisenhower, "More than a military man, he was a statesman who was on intimate terms with most of Europe's leaders, was trusted, liked, and admired almost to the point of adulation by all of them." Organizationally, Eisenhower pushed forward with the development of integrated defense plans for the allies, with the corresponding expansion of NATO's military bureaucracy.[14] For the rest of the Cold War, all viewed the SACEUR as NATO's single most influential official, although the individual SACEURs varied in the degree of influence they exercised within the alliance.[15]

Despite the exceptional transatlantic support for Eisenhower, the allies still felt a need for improved organizational leadership and enhanced political integration. Before his appointment as NATO's first secretary general, Lord Hastings Lionel Ismay had less than positive impressions of NATO's "organization," referring to a NATO meeting in 1952 as a "milling mob." In his memoirs, Secretary of State Dean Acheson also characterized NATO in its first years as "a body—or more accurately twelve bodies—without a head."[16] At its

---

14. Stephen E. Ambrose with Morris Honick, "Eisenhower: Rekindling the Spirit of the West," in *Generals in International Politics,* ed. Robert S. Jordan (Lexington, KY: University Press of Kentucky, 1987), 11; Gregory W. Pedlow, "The Politics of NATO Command 1950–1962," in *U.S. Military Forces in Europe,* ed. Simon W. Duke and Wolfgang Krieger (Boulder, CO: Westview Press, 1993), 15–42. See also Robert E. Osgood, *Alliances and American Foreign Policy* (Baltimore, MD: Johns Hopkins University Press, 1968), 49; and Alexander M. Bielakowski, "Eisenhower: The First SACEUR," *War and Society* 22, no. 2 (2004): 95–108.

15. Robert Hunter, *Security in Europe* (Bloomington, IN: Indiana University Press, 1969), 61–62. Among all the SACEURs who served during the Cold War, Lauris Norstad is viewed as the most influential. See Robert S. Jordan, *Norstad: Cold War NATO Supreme Allied Commander* (New York: St. Martin's Press, 2000).

16. Hastings Lionel Ismay, *The Memoirs of General Lord Ismay* (New York: Viking Press, 1960), 458; Acheson, quoted in Jordan, *Political Leadership in NATO,* 8.

Lisbon meeting in February 1952, NATO sought to rectify this problem through the creation of the civilian position of secretary general to provide political guidance and leadership to the alliance. Since NATO operates by consensus, each member state still had veto power over all decisions, but when acting on behalf of a specific NAC decision, the secretary general could provide political guidance to NATO's military authorities, including the SACEUR. Given the United States' tremendous influence in the alliance, due primarily to its military superiority, the American general serving as SACEUR retained considerable political influence among the allies. The alliance also created an international civilian staff to support the secretary general in providing the necessary organizational unity and enhanced cooperation.

Some disagreement existed between the United Kingdom and the United States over the appropriate role of the new civilian leadership. The British preferred an institutional leader with limited powers and only a small staff. They sought a leader with little "political" power in shaping the alliance. In contrast, the United States wanted a secretary general who could oversee meetings of and introduce issues to the North Atlantic Council. In the American view, the leader would have a staff of specialists who would improve the knowledge base available at NATO—and, it was hoped, improve the coordination among allied states and their ambassadors. Much of the United States' proposal won out, but in exchange the United States agreed to British general Lord Ismay to serve as the first secretary general. The little formal organization that did exist was transferred to Paris at Palais de Chaillot, where NATO headquarters remained until 1967. Lord Ismay became NATO's first secretary general on April 4, 1952, NATO's third anniversary, and the practice of having a European secretary general took root.[17]

HASTINGS LIONEL ISMAY, 1952–1957

As with nearly all Cold War secretaries general, Lord Hastings Lionel Ismay was considered an exceptional diplomat, and he brought

17. Kaplan, *The United States and NATO,* 169; Kay, *NATO and the Future of European Security,* 36.

an extensive background in military and international affairs to NATO. Most analysts concur, however, that as NATO's first secretary general, much like his Cold War successors, Lord Ismay was nonetheless seriously constrained by the allies when it came to dealing with the major foreign policy questions of the day.

Regarding his leadership legacy, historians credit Ismay with developing a professional international staff and the necessary organizational committees to support the alliance. In many respects, Ismay helped create the needed infrastructure to make the transatlantic alliance thrive. When Ismay became secretary general, the Council of Deputies was also replaced with permanent representatives at the ambassadorial rank who officially conducted the business of the North Atlantic Council as the principal decision-making body for the alliance, and who remained in permanent session. This council remains today. Ismay was also provided with a deputy secretary general to support him; this position also remains today. In implementing the additional reforms that followed, Ismay was quite successful and helped build and improve upon NATO's organizational legitimacy as a multilateral military alliance.[18]

It is notable, however, that the office of the secretary general was especially weak in its infancy. The secretary general did not automatically chair North Atlantic Council meetings; only in the absence of its chairman did Ismay assert what he felt was his right to oversee a meeting, which was accepted by the allies. In 1955, the NAC granted the secretary general the authority to chair all its meetings. But, although the secretary general did begin chairing the NAC sessions, he had no vote in them—and still does not. The secretary general also was not allowed to speak on issues unless specifically authorized to do so by the council. Had Ismay chosen to ignore such rules, he would have greatly limited his own leadership legitimacy among the allies.[19] Ismay succeeded in fostering much-needed organization in NATO, but his position's formal authority was weak from the beginning.

Ismay was also an important player in making sure that another

18. Robert S. Jordan, *The NATO International Staff/Secretariat 1952–1957* (London: Oxford University Press, 1967). See also M. Margaret Ball, *NATO and the European Union Movement* (London: Stevens and Sons, 1959), 58.

19. Jordan, *Political Leadership in NATO*, 45, 293.

American general replaced Eisenhower as the next SACEUR. At this time, in April 1952, it was not necessarily determined that the SACEUR would always be from the United States, as tradition dictates today. Although this was not a point of major contention among the allies, the United States was clear in its intent to appoint a second American as SACEUR.[20] Ismay, who consulted privately with all the ambassadors at NATO, ensured that the Truman administration's choice of General Matthew B. Ridgway would be approved unanimously when Eisenhower left the SACEUR position to begin his American presidential campaign.[21] It is worth noting that Ismay's ability to lead, both in making his infrastructural improvements, as well as in his role in securing a second American SACEUR, was due partly to strong American support, which is always an important factor in the ability of the secretaries general to shape decisions for the alliance, as will be demonstrated in the chapters that follow.

In his role as secretary general, Lord Ismay viewed himself as a servant of the NAC. He preferred quiet diplomacy within NATO. He also preferred that NAC meetings be kept short. His role in these settings was to summarize viewpoints and bring the meetings to a close. In the council meetings, he was not a policy entrepreneur who pushed his own agenda onto the member states, although he is certainly viewed as a secretary general who could help identify consensus positions among the allies in times of disagreement.[22]

Although Ismay played an important role in creating NATO's organizational structure, which has had a long-lasting impact on the alliance, it must also be recognized that serious limitations existed on his ability to lead the alliance. Ismay first took office when Dwight Eisenhower served as SACEUR. Not only did Eisenhower have an extraordinary international reputation, but also he utilized his excellent diplomatic skills quite effectively among European political and military leaders, which continued to heighten his stature at NATO.[23] Ismay served with Eisenhower for only a few weeks,

20. George Eugene Pelletier, "Ridgway," in *Generals in International Politics,* ed. Robert S. Jordan (Lexington: University Press of Kentucky, 1987), 37.

21. Jordan, *Political Leadership in NATO,* 44.

22. Ibid., 34–35.

23. See Stephen E. Ambrose with Morris Honick, "Eisenhower: Rekindling the Spirit of the West," 8–30.

but the practice of having a strong SACEUR leading the alliance had been established under him. Although Eisenhower's replacement, General Ridgway, did not have status or diplomatic skills akin to Eisenhower's, the precedent of a strong SACEUR was in place. Ridgway was not received as warmly as Eisenhower had been (no one would have been), perhaps in part because of the photo of Ridgway that was circulated internationally when his appointment as SACEUR was announced in May 1952: in the photo, Ridgway wore his steel helmet and two grenades attached to his uniform, an image some Europeans translated as forthcoming military aggression. Ridgway, who was not a favorite of the newly elected Eisenhower administration, was replaced with General Alfred M. Greunther in 1953, after only fourteen months as SACEUR. Yet, during his tenure, Ridgway was still immersed in difficult political challenges for the alliance, including the rearming of West Germany through the European Defense Community proposal, as well as the establishment of a new southern command to accommodate the new members of the alliance, Greece and Turkey, which were admitted in 1952.[24] Although Ridgway initially viewed his role as limited to "military" affairs, it is clear that he played a very "political" role at NATO because of the questions in play during his tenure, which provides additional evidence of an influential SACEUR.

Ismay also served alongside General Greunther, who was President Eisenhower's first selection as SACEUR. Greunther was more popularly received by the Europeans than Ridgway because of his close personal relationship with Eisenhower, his previous service as chief of staff to both Eisenhower and Ridgway while each served as SACEUR, and his more polished diplomatic skills as compared with Ridgway's. At the same time, by 1955 and certainly by 1956, Greunther was actively seeking retirement from the military, just as Ismay's political stature was growing within the alliance. This period is one in which the secretary general exercised a bit more influence within the alliance as compared with the SACEUR, although given Greunther's close and widely known friendship with Eisenhower, coupled with his considerable diplomatic skills, it would be incorrect to suggest a "weak" SACEUR; rather, there was a "strengthened" secretary general at this time. This increase in power, how-

24. Pelletier, "Ridgway," 39, 46–49.

ever, did not last long, as Greunther's successor, Lauris Norstad, quickly reclaimed the SACEUR's dominant leadership role at NATO.[25]

Another critical event of note during Ismay's leadership tenure, which reflected NATO's and the secretary general's own inability to promote consultation, was the difference of opinion over actions surrounding the Suez Canal crisis of 1956. After Egypt temporarily nationalized the canal, on October 31, 1956, France, the United Kingdom, and Israel launched military strikes on Egypt. These attacks had been planned covertly in advance, absent consultation with the North Atlantic Council. The military actions generated vigorous American opposition and, ironically, found the United States and the Soviet Union in agreement. While the political elite in France, the United Kingdom, and the United States all understood that each state had different reasons and interests for acting in the manner they did, the event demonstrated the true absence of consultation among the allies as well as the NAC's impotence at the time, especially given that the allies had defined their national interests in such dramatically different terms. As an institution, NATO was left as a bystander in the crisis.[26]

Prior to the Suez Canal crisis, sensing the growing political divide and the absence of consultation among the alliance's major players, Lord Ismay encouraged discussions in the NAC that highlighted the need for improved means of consultation. The challenge was taken up at NATO's 1956 spring ministerial by the foreign ministers of Canada, Italy, and Norway (Lester Pearson, Halvard Lange, and Gaetano Martino), who later became known as "the Three Wise Men." In their eventual report to the NAC, which noted that the

25. On Greunther's reception as SACEUR, see Robert S. Jordan, "Greunther: Attempts to Retain NATO Solidarity," in *Generals in International Politics*, 53–72. On this elevation in influence for the secretary general, see Robert S. Jordan, "Norstad," in *Generals in International Politics*, 74.

26. These events, within the context of NATO, are best addressed in Douglas Stuart and William Tow, *The Limits of Alliance: NATO Out-of-Area Problems since 1949* (Baltimore, MD: Johns Hopkins University Press, 1990), 58–66. See also M. Margaret Ball, *NATO and the European Union Movement*, 50; Jordan, *Political Leadership in NATO*, 37; and Hans J. Morgenthau, "The Crisis of the Alliance," in *NATO in Quest of Cohesion*, ed. Karl H. Cerny and Henry W. Briefs (New York: Frederick A. Praeger, 1965), 129.

alliance had "undergone severe strains," their recommendations called generally for a reconfirmation of the alliance's collective defense principles and a recommitment to political cooperation. More specifically, their report advocated for a stronger secretary general who could now formally propose methods to improve consultation within the alliance, and who would also oversee all NAC meetings. The allies were also encouraged to keep the secretary general informed of all issues within the alliance.[27]

The NAC accepted the recommendations from the Three Wise Men, but at the same time some members, especially the United Kingdom and the United States, viewed the recommendations with some suspicion. Given these two states' leadership roles in NATO, their reservations were significant; consequently, a substantial change in the secretary general's powers did not take place. The Three Wise Men's report, however, was still critical in that it encouraged Paul-Henri Spaak to become Ismay's successor and NATO's second secretary general.[28]

PAUL-HENRI SPAAK, 1957–1961

Belgian Paul-Henri Spaak, who had served previously in his home government as prime minister and foreign minister, became secretary general on May 16, 1957. Like Lord Ismay, Spaak brought extensive experience in international affairs to the office of secretary general. He also brought with him a new view of what the appropriate role for the secretary general should be in the alliance. In contrast to Ismay, Spaak sought to exercise political, policy-making, and public leadership of the alliance, and he did not shy away from asserting his views in NAC meetings. Spaak wanted NATO to broaden its scope, especially into areas of shared economic concern among the allies.[29]

Historians credit Spaak with having exceptional oratorical skills and with being a tireless advocate of transatlantic consultation and

27. See Jordan, *NATO International Staff/Secretariat*, 292–93.
28. Stuart and Tow, *Limits of Alliance*, 64–65; Jordan, *Political Leadership in NATO*, 62.
29. Jordan, *Political Leadership in NATO*, 62–72.

cooperation. At the same time, the political constraints placed on his ability to lead severely limited his influence. When Spaak sought to identify himself as NATO's principal spokesperson, he was not supported by most of the NAC. To a large extent, he was also ignored by General Lauris Norstad, who served as SACEUR during the entire period of Spaak's leadership. When policy leaks to the media came from NATO and were published, NATO policy makers asked Norstad about the accuracy of the reports—not Spaak. Norstad had exceptional organizational skills, engaged in all debates across the alliance, and spoke on behalf of the alliance when he desired. At times, Spaak also found himself at odds with the U.S. ambassador to NATO, W. Randolph Burgess.[30]

Spaak served as secretary general during the political reemergence of General Charles de Gaulle, who became president of France's Fifth Republic in 1958. De Gaulle's arrival and his penchant for French nationalism severely impeded Spaak's ability to lead NATO and affected all secretaries general that served contemporaneously with him. In expressing France's concerns about the United States' eminence in nuclear weaponry among the allies in 1958, de Gaulle addressed the United States and the United Kingdom (not the NAC) in calling for a "triumvirate" that would make nuclear decisions jointly for the alliance. In doing so, de Gaulle openly displayed his disregard for the NAC and, implicitly, for the secretary general. Spaak openly opposed de Gaulle's proposal, which essentially led to a political divorce between the two. As France became more independent in its foreign policy, Spaak's already limited influence weakened. Being an activist secretary general who was not supported by most in the NAC, coupled with the hypernationalism of de Gaulle's France and the dominating presence of General Norstad, made for an especially difficult era for Spaak as he struggled to find ways to improve alliance consultation. Spaak resigned in 1961 with much personal disappointment about his leadership tenure and about NATO more generally. It is reported that, upon his resignation, Spaak lobbied quietly for an American to serve as secretary general, since he felt that NATO's credibility was then in

30. Francis A. Beer, *Integration and Disintegration in NATO* (Columbus, OH: Ohio State University Press, 1969), 30; Jordan, *Political Leadership in NATO*, 48–49, 73, 82–83.

crisis. It seems that in his view, only an American leader could reaffirm NATO's leadership role in transatlantic security.[31]

DIRK STIKKER, 1961–1964

Like Spaak's, Dirk Stikker's leadership as secretary general was affected negatively by President de Gaulle. Stikker served previously as foreign minister for his country, the Netherlands, and as the Dutch ambassador to the United Kingdom. In 1958, he was given a dual appointment by his government to serve as its ambassador to NATO and to the Organization for European Economic Cooperation, where he remained until his selection as secretary general.

Unfortunately, Stikker entered the alliance under difficult political circumstances, which plagued most of his leadership tenure. In the political process and internal negotiations that took place when NATO was selecting Spaak's replacement—a process in which the allied governments suggested and lobbied for potential candidates for the position and that essentially remains the same process today—Stikker was the clearly favored candidate until France expressed its support for Manlio Brosio, then Italian ambassador to the United States. With open American and British support for Stikker, the Italians dropped their backing of Brosio, and the French were isolated without their favored candidate. In recognizing its defeat, France then moved to support Stikker, and alliance consensus was reached.[32]

France's change in position, however, was not a defeat for French nationalism. Upon his selection as secretary general, Stikker reached out to all allied governments and sought meetings with all chief executives. For three months de Gaulle did not respond to Stikker's request to meet. When the meeting finally did occur, it lasted no more than twenty-five minutes, and it was the last meeting ever to occur between the two. De Gaulle also refused to see Stikker when the secretary general resigned in 1964. Similarly, Stikker spoke only

31. Jordan, *Political Leadership in NATO*, 76–94; Beer, *Integration and Disintegration in NATO*, 34.
32. Jordan, *Political Leadership in NATO*, 166–67.

once with the French foreign minister, Maurice Couve de Mur-ville.[33]

Stikker, who had suffered from poor health in his previous ambassadorial appointments, also became ill while serving at NATO and was periodically unable to oversee alliance business. His occasional absences hurt him tremendously, especially with small states that rely upon their personal access to the secretary general to have their voices heard more effectively by the major powers. Moreover, before Stikker's tenure the small states' ambassadors had met in weekly informal lunch settings, where no minutes were kept and conversations were held in confidence. These "Tuesday luncheons" were a way for ambassadors to air issues without the formal oversight of their respective governments, and to get a sense of other allies' perspectives. In contrast, Stikker felt that views could be expressed best in the traditional formats, so he did not promote or attend these meetings. His absence from the luncheons further diminished his ability to influence NATO's agenda. Like Spaak, Stikker was also overshadowed by the influence of the SACEUR, General Lauris Norstad, who is viewed by many as the most influential of all Cold War SACEURs. Norstad's dominating presence clearly limited the individual impact Stikker could make as secretary general.[34]

Although Stikker had excellent knowledge of defense issues, and was well received by the United States during his tenure as secretary general, French nationalism severely impeded the enhancement of consultation and cooperation during his time at NATO. Stikker's memoirs openly criticize de Gaulle and his "French Grandeur," and his animosity toward the French in general is unmistakable.[35] His performance shows once more the political limitations borne by NATO's secretaries general. In the face of direct opposition from one of the allies, especially a powerful member like France, the secretary general can find his office nearly powerless in promoting consensus.

33. Stikker did have better relations with France's defense minister, Pierre Messmer (ibid., 130–31).

34. Ibid., 127–34.

35. Dirk U. Stikker, *Men of Responsibility* (New York: Harper and Row, 1965), 352–56. See also Sloan, *NATO, the European Union, and the Atlantic Community,* 42–47.

MANLIO BROSIO, 1964–1971

Manlio Brosio, the Italian ambassador to France in 1964, who had served previously in similar capacities in Washington, London, and the Soviet Union, and earlier as Italian minister of defense and deputy prime minister, became NATO's fourth secretary general on August 1, 1964. Brosio was a skillful and cautious diplomat who in a number of respects expanded the degree of consultation within the alliance and also managed several difficult issues during his tenure adeptly. In terms of his achievements as secretary general, Brosio truly stands out when compared to his predecessors. Yet, owing again to President de Gaulle's French nationalism, Brosio, too, was limited in what influence he could exercise.

Unlike Secretary General Spaak, Brosio employed considerable self-restraint in his leadership approach. Through his congenial yet meticulous personality, Brosio demanded that NAC sessions always remain professional, with close attention to and respect for proper diplomatic etiquette. Like Stikker, Brosio was well versed on defense issues; he would arrive early to NATO headquarters to read the morning newspapers and, reportedly, to read all NATO documents that reached his office. During his leadership tenure, which he began at age sixty-seven, he also studied German, feeling that his German language skills were not adequate for the position of secretary general. In contrast to Stikker, Brosio made a conscious effort to promote the off-the-record Tuesday luncheons among the ambassadors. He attended the luncheons and encouraged the ambassadors to speak freely about alliance policies and their own governments' positions. In this regard, part of his leadership success was due to the confidence and trust that he quickly earned as secretary general.[36] As will be demonstrated in later chapters, this factor can be a critical (but certainly intangible) element of effective leadership at NATO. Manfred Wörner and especially Javier Solana owe part of their leadership success to similar "personal" leadership aspects of their diplomatic approaches.

As secretary general, Brosio worked well with all of the NATO ambassadors. He had an especially good relationship with the American ambassador, Harlan Cleveland, who notes in his mem-

36. Jordan, *Political Leadership in NATO,* 174–87.

oirs that Brosio's support could provide that "priceless ingredient of the political mix," a comment that clearly indicates Brosio's importance in fostering alliance consensus. Cleveland also credits Brosio with having played a positive role for the alliance in 1967 in ameliorating tensions between Turkey and Greece over the governance of Cyprus. The trust that he earned from the allies was also especially useful in finding consensus in the NAC, as he was unusually skilled in finding semantical nuances that permitted the allies to find agreement in the NAC's written memoranda. Because of his extensive reading and preparation, he had excellent command of the policy issues in question. If, during a NAC session, an ambassador surprised Brosio with a proposal that he knew would not have the allies' full support, Brosio would immediately call for a five-minute recess to meet with the dissident ambassador. More often than not, when the NAC reconvened, the ambassador would withdraw the flawed proposal.[37]

Of the events during Brosio's tenure, however, two stand out in terms of his legacy. On July 1, 1966, President Charles de Gaulle requested that NATO remove all of its military installations from France within one year and also requested France's removal from NATO's integrated military command. In addition to the concerns he had expressed previously on American nuclear power within the alliance, and his preference for a "triumvirate" decision-making approach on the use of nuclear weapons, which the United States opposed, de Gaulle maintained that NATO's deployment of troops on French soil represented a violation of French sovereignty, and he argued that the integrated command (whose mission is joint military planning) could potentially engage France in a war in which it did not wish to fight. Historians also maintain that American policy differences in France's colonial war with Algeria and American opposition to France's role in the Suez Canal crisis created larger suspicions in France that the United States would not necessarily come to France's defense if it was attacked. At the same time, de Gaulle did not remove French troops from Germany, nor did he prevent

37. Harlan Cleveland, *NATO: The Transatlantic Bargain* (New York: Harper and Row, 1970), 56. See also Jordan, *Political Leadership in NATO*, 182, 188, 206, 212. Stanton Burnett, former U.S. State Department official at NATO, phone interview with author, May 31, 2005.

the allies from using French air space in any NATO training missions. He also authorized joint military training operations with NATO troops in Germany, and he did not call for France's removal from alliance political consultations.[38]

In response to de Gaulle's demands, Brosio purposefully faded into the background and allowed the Belgian ambassador to NATO, André de Staercke, to essentially provide temporary political leadership of the alliance. Since Brosio viewed himself as secretary general to all of NATO's allies, he felt it would be inappropriate to exercise leadership given the intra-alliance differences over how to respond to de Gaulle's demands. In order to keep the allies functioning in light of France's demands, de Staercke held meetings with the other fourteen allies (also known as *les quatorze*) at his office and his apartment in Paris if necessary, which Brosio actively supported. The secretary general attended the meetings, but did not exercise his normal chairmanship duties. At these meetings, with eventual French approval, the allies agreed that France would not participate formally in meetings of NATO's Defense Planning Committee.[39]

Although an argument could be made that Brosio was somewhat passive toward France in 1966, in retrospect some historians credit him with helping to keep NATO together under difficult circumstances. Given his continued efforts to work with France and President de Gaulle from the moment he became secretary general, it appears that he did everything possible to contain French nationalism. Brosio maintained excellent diplomatic relations with France, never openly criticized de Gaulle, and is viewed as being helpful in the transition to NATO's new headquarters in Belgium. He also played a critical role in strengthening the Defense Planning Committee, which he felt was necessary to maintain NATO's deterrent value against the Soviet Union after the French had removed them-

---

38. Samuel F. Wells Jr., "Charles de Gaulle and the French Withdrawal from NATO's Integrated Command," in *American Historians and the Atlantic Alliance*, ed. Lawrence S. Kaplan (Kent, OH: Kent State University Press, 1991), 81–94; Michael M. Harrison, *The Reluctant Ally: France and Atlantic Security* (Baltimore, MD: Johns Hopkins University Press, 1981); Cleveland, *The Transatlantic Bargain*, 103.

39. Jordan, *Political Leadership in NATO*, 196–200; Cleveland, *The Transatlantic Bargain*, 106.

selves from the committee.[40] As is addressed in Chapter 5, this committee took on heightened importance in the 2003 debate over Iraq. The second major feature of Brosio's legacy is his usefulness in promoting consensus when the alliance issued its historic Harmel Report, although Brosio personally had great reservations about its contents. Named after the Belgian foreign minister, Pierre Harmel, who led the call in encouraging NATO's reevaluation, the report was issued in December 1967, after a year of discussion on the future purposes of the alliance. Division had grown among NATO members, with some feeling that the alliance should do more to promote diplomatic strategies to end the Cold War. The Harmel Report called for NATO to assume two primary missions: defense and détente. In short, the report encouraged the allies to continue with their military modernization efforts, but also to recognize that arms-control efforts and confidence-building measures should be encouraged with the Soviet Union.[41]

In the short term, the Harmel Report appeared to have some impact on the alliance. The Nixon administration engaged in arms-control negotiations with the Soviets through the Anti-Ballistic Missile Treaty and the Strategic Arms Limitation Talks, but in 1975, President Gerald Ford indicated that American "détente" policies would not imply any weakening of military defenses or a discontinuation of necessary military investments to protect the United States and its allies.[42] In addition, in 1979 former U.S. secretary of state Henry Kissinger noted in a speech in Brussels that NATO had little room for détente. Kissinger's comments took many Europeans by surprise and did little to advance transatlantic unity at the time. But in

40. Jordan, *Political Leadership in NATO*, 198–201; Beer, *Integration and Disintegration in NATO*, 125; Lawrence S. Kaplan, *NATO and the United States: The Enduring Alliance* (Boston: Twayne, 1988), 124.

41. See Bruna Bagnato, "NATO in the Mid-Sixties: The View of Secretary General Manlio Brosio" (paper presented at the International Conference, Parallel History Project on NATO and the Warsaw Pact, Zurich, August 25–28, 2004); Jordan, *Political Leadership in NATO*, 214.

42. Sloan, *NATO, the European Union, and the Atlantic Community*, 50. See also Joan Hoff-Wilson, "'Nixongerism,' NATO, and Détente," in *American Historians and the Atlantic Alliance*, ed. Lawrence S. Kaplan (Kent, OH: Kent State University Press, 1991); and Gerald R. Ford, "Address in Minneapolis before the Annual Convention of the American Legion," *Public Papers of the Presidents*, August 19, 1975, 1171–78.

retrospect, other analysts have noted the importance of the Harmel Report in changing and widening NATO's mission at the appropriate time. The report helped maintain alliance unity, as a number of European allies felt that NATO had moved too far from diplomatic solutions to resolve the Cold War. Some of the European allies were also worried that the United States would ignore their interests when it pursued its bilateral arms-control policies with the Soviet Union. The Harmel Report clearly identified some common interests and strengthened transatlantic support for NATO.[43] Thus, on these two policy fronts Brosio had an impact on NATO and succeeded in promoting transatlantic consensus.

At the same time, it must be recognized that much of Brosio's leadership success came in response to serious political crises *within* NATO, which dealt with debates among the allies. Brosio was adept at averting additional crises and preventing more serious diplomatic tensions within the NAC. Yet because of differences among NATO's members, the secretary general was certainly limited in what he could do in terms of actual policy developments for the alliance. On France's decision to withdraw from NATO's military command in 1966, General Lauris Norstad, who was no longer SACEUR, noted to the U.S. Congress, "We have clearly moved from disarray to dissension to crisis. Let me emphasize and reemphasize that this is a crisis, because we have been told in recent weeks that this is just another minor incident in the course of a long life of NATO. It is in fact a crisis."[44] As it had with Spaak's and Stikker's potential for leadership, France's position toward NATO limited NATO itself and, by extension, Brosio's ability to lead.

Brosio was himself careful to keep NATO's mission and purpose limited. He held the view that NATO should not go out of area, that is, beyond the allies' borders, and in this respect he did not support initiatives to take NATO into uncharted political territory. Brosio helped to keep NATO's objectives narrow, which, for better or for worse, meant that he would not encourage or pursue novel initiatives. Such views led some at NATO to conclude that Brosio was

---

43. Sloan, *NATO, the European Union, and the Atlantic Community,* 47–52, 57; Lawrence S. Kaplan, *NATO Divided, NATO United: The Evolution of an Alliance* (Westport, CT: Praeger, 2004), especially chap. 4.

44. Norstad, quoted in Beer, *Integration and Disintegration in NATO,* 257.

"extremely" cautious if not "excessively" cautious as secretary general. Moreover, it is noteworthy that the calls for the Harmel Report first came from the Canadian government in 1964. Two years later, Harmel issued his call for a NATO study, which was then acted upon by the allies and eventually released in December 1967.[45] This cautious and slow approach is not surprising given Brosio's natural leadership tendencies and his general skepticism of détente.

Brosio worked alongside two SACEURs, General Lyman L. Lemnitzer and General Andrew J. Goodpaster. Lemnitzer viewed his SACEUR leadership role as being in "military" affairs only, somewhat akin to the view of General Greunther, which again limited the SACEUR's influence and willingness to engage in "political" leadership of the alliance. Such an approach was markedly different from General Norstad's. Yet Lemnitzer was cognizant of the power, authority, and history of NATO's strong SACEUR, and still worked to project that image. Lemnitzer and Brosio did not develop a close personal relationship, a fact due in part to Lemnitzer's views on the dominant status of the SACEUR, yet they still managed to form a cooperative working relationship.[46] Lemnitzer's authority was also clearly damaged by de Gaulle's "extraction" decision in 1966. De Gaulle demonstrated in a profound way that neither Brosio nor Lemnitzer had much ability to control France, and thus both the SACEUR and the secretary general suffered politically during this time.[47]

As SACEUR, General Goodpaster played a more political role within the alliance and regained some of the political influence that had been weakened under Lemnitzer's leadership in the position. Brosio found it easier to work with Goodpaster, who shared his views on détente, and, like Brosio, was also an advocate for increased defense spending from all the NATO allies.[48]

Leadership can clearly come in different forms. Brosio did much

45. See Jordan, *Political Leadership in NATO*, 174, and Beer, *Integration and Disintegration in NATO*, 36, 40–41.

46. Jordan, *Political Leadership in NATO*, 226.

47. On Lemnitzer specifically, see Lawrence S. Kaplan and Kathleen A. Kellner, "Lemnitzer: Surviving the French Military Withdrawal," in *Generals in International Politics*, ed. Robert S. Jordan (Lexington, KY: University Press of Kentucky, 1987).

48. Jordan, *Political Leadership in NATO*, 231–32.

through his reserved diplomatic approach to advance transatlantic consensus. He exercised leadership by keeping NATO's mission limited, through his quiet mediating efforts, and through his meticulous preparation on all policy matters, all at a time when political differences within the alliance truly threatened NATO's credibility. Because of the exhausting demands of being secretary general, he requested his own departure and relinquished his office on September 3, 1971.

Joseph Luns, 1971–1984

Joseph Luns, a former Dutch foreign minister, became NATO's secretary general on October 1, 1971, and remained in office until June 24, 1984, serving the longest term ever in the position. When it became known that Brosio intended to retire, Luns campaigned quietly and successfully, and secured the nomination before the issue of Brosio's successor ever became an issue. Luns occupied the office during difficult times for the alliance, when, in the latter years of his leadership, American and Soviet tensions were especially high. Moreover, American administrations were playing the lead role in arms-control negotiations with the Soviet Union, and in many respects NATO increasingly became an extension of American foreign policy, rather than a consultative framework for the development of policy.[49]

One example of the political environment early in Luns's service at NATO, and of the United States' lukewarm commitment to the alliance at the time, is evident in the memoirs of James K. Bartleman, former Canadian ambassador to NATO, when he discusses David Bruce, who served as the American ambassador to NATO from November 1974 to January 1976, early in Luns's tenure. Bruce had a long and distinguished career in American diplomacy, having served as U.S. ambassador to France, West Germany, the United Kingdom, and China, as well as undersecretary of state under President Truman. Bruce, however, was born on February 12, 1898, and thus became U.S. ambassador to NATO at the age of seventy-six. According to Bartleman, Ambassador Bruce was "a septuagenarian

---

49. Burnett interview, May 31, 2005; Thomas H. Etzold, "The Military Role of NATO," in *NATO after Thirty Years*, ed. Lawrence S. Kaplan and Robert W. Clawson (Wilmington, DE: Scholarly Resources, 1981).

past his prime . . . who had to rely on cue cards in the cut and thrust of council debate." Bruce's biographer adds that Bruce suffered from poor health while in Brussels, and that he found his responsibilities "tedious." The official business at NATO bored him. He much preferred the more leisurely ambassadorship in China.[50] The fact that the United States would appoint someone with such a lack of interest in the projects of NATO ostensibly shows its disregard for the importance of the alliance during those years.

During his entire tenure at NATO, Luns was considered a vigorous backer of the United States. As he had in his previous role as the Netherlands' foreign minister, which had lasted for a record nineteen years, Luns brought his passionate ideological conservatism with him to Brussels. Henry Kissinger points out in his memoirs that Luns was "a staunch friend of the United States," so much so that his passionate support of the Americans occasionally brought "snickers" from other European diplomats. Another reflection of Luns's American sympathies was evident during Kissinger's last trip to Brussels in December 1976, when Luns said of him, "You will stand in history as one of the most effective foreign ministers of our century. . . . May I summarize our common feeling by quoting Shakespeare: 'He was a man, take him for all in all, I shall not look upon his like again.'"[51]

Like his predecessors, Luns is credited with being a skilled diplomat who conducted NAC meetings with considerable authority. Luns's diplomatic style, especially in his early years as secretary general, was confrontational, as he attempted to "bully" into submission those ambassadors who disagreed with the United States' vision of transatlantic unity.[52] Luns, who stood six feet, seven inches

50. James K. Bartleman, *On Six Continents: A Life in Canada's Foreign Service* (Toronto: McClelland and Stewart, 2004), 80; Nelson D. Lankford, *The Last American Aristocrat: The Biography of David K. E. Bruce, 1898–1977* (Boston: Little, Brown, 1996), 392.

51. Henry Kissinger, *Years of Upheaval* (Boston: Little, Brown, 1982), 182. It has been noted by others that Luns was "seemingly uncritical of US foreign policy" ("Consummate Diplomat Who Believed in Europe," http://www.rnw.nl/hotspots/html/lunsobit.html). Luns, quoted in Walter Isaacson, *Kissinger: A Biography* (New York: Simon and Schuster, 1992), 704.

52. Burnett interview, May 31, 2005; David M. Abshire, *Preventing World War III* (New York: Harper and Row, 1988), 22, 173. See also Kissinger, *Years of Upheaval*, 722; and Jamie Shea, "Obituary: Joseph Luns," NATO, http://www.nato.int/docu/review/2002/issue2/english/obituary.html.

tall, occupied a tremendous political and physical stature. He was well liked at NATO headquarters and interacted well with political and military officials at all levels.[53]

In sharp contrast to Brosio, Luns ran NAC sessions very informally, referring to ambassadors by their first names during the meetings. He also would consistently remove his shoes at the beginning of each NAC session. Moreover, Luns was quite different from Brosio in his understanding of the political and military nuances of NATO issues under consideration. Luns enjoyed all "political" and ceremonial roles of being NATO's secretary general, but often chose to rely upon his past knowledge of issues and his own perceived ability to charm (or bulldoze when necessary) allies who were preventing consensus. In this respect, he was far less prepared and educated on the policy issues of the day than was Brosio. Luns could still find ways to promote consensus, but NAC sessions were far more unpredictable than they had been in the Brosio era.[54]

Luns's absence from nearly all histories of NATO and the infrequent references to his leadership role by his contemporaries is striking, especially considering the length of his term in office. General Alexander Haig, who served as SACEUR from December 15, 1974, to June 29, 1979, as well as U.S. secretary of state for the first two years of the Reagan administration, mentions Luns only once in his memoirs. Haig notes that Luns pleaded with him upon his arrival as SACEUR to encourage the Dutch Armed Forces to cut their hair, shave their beards, and iron their uniforms. It should be added that Haig was an especially strong and well-respected SACEUR, who earned political support from the Europeans because of his excellent consultative skills. He also had strong policy interests and in this regard had another leadership advantage over Luns. Similar to Haig, Cyrus Vance, who served as U.S. secretary of state in the Carter administration from 1977 to 1980, discusses NATO on a number of occasions in his memoirs, but includes no mention of Luns.[55]

The Soviet Union's decision on December 25, 1979, to invade

53. Dan Cougil, former U.S. Department of Defense official at NATO, interview with author, June 17, 2003. See also Shea, "Obituary: Joseph Luns."

54. Burnett interview, May 31, 2005.

55. Alexander M. Haig Jr. with Charles McCarry, *Inner Circles: How America Changed the World: A Memoir* (New York: Warner Books, 1992), 523–24; Morris

Afghanistan presents a telling case of NATO's inability to find common ground, despite even the dire actions of its primary nemesis. It is noteworthy first that little consensus existed in determining how to respond to the Soviets' military action, and then that NATO was very slow in its response to the Soviet invasion: it took three weeks for NATO to discuss the Soviet invasion. The responses from Europe varied widely. Recalling in 1983 the allies' reactions and summarizing the ongoing problems that he saw at NATO, former U.S. secretary of state Cyrus Vance wrote,

> We must understand that consultation is more than merely listening to what one's fellow members have to say. We must be willing not only to discuss matters thoroughly in advance, but also to adjust our position in order to achieve a unified alliance position. If we do this, we will remove an important cause of the strains that now beset the alliance. . . . If the alliance is to remain the foundation of Western security there must be basic agreement on the nature of our global objectives and on the collective responsibility of the West to protect its interests.[56]

Another evident policy divide was over the Europeans' unwillingness to support the aggressive U.S. economic sanctions directed against the Soviet Union. While Europe remained focused on détente, both the Carter and Reagan administrations moved steadily toward policies stressing greater confrontation and military modernization. Such policies, and especially President Ronald Reagan's increased defense expenditures, created widespread opposition and protests across Europe.[57]

In contrast to European sentiment at the time, Luns is remembered for being an advocate for strong defense policies and military invest-

---

Honick, "Haig: The Diplomacy of Allied Command," *Generals in International Politics*, 151–74; Burnett interview, May 31, 2005; Cyrus Vance, *Hard Choices* (New York: Simon and Schuster, 1983).

56. Vance, *Hard Choices*, 393–94. See also Dan Smith, *Pressure: How America Runs NATO* (London: Bloomsbury, 1989), 20.

57. Sloan, *NATO, the European Union, and the Atlantic Community*, 51; Linda P. Brady, "NATO in the 1980s: An Uncertain Future?" in *NATO in the 1980s: Challenges and Responses*, ed. Linda P. Brady and Joyce P. Kaufman (New York: Praeger, 1985), 4; Gaddis Smith, "The SS–20 Challenge and Opportunity: The Dual Track Decision and Its Consequences, 1977–1983," in *American Historians and the Atlantic Alliance*, ed. Lawrence S. Kaplan (Kent, OH: Kent State University Press, 1991), 132.

ment in Europe.[58] While Luns was respected for his quick wit, charm, and advocacy for NATO and transatlantic cooperation, his ideological leaning toward the United States surely marginalized his ability to generate wider diplomatic support. Those associated with NATO frequently note Luns's regal flair and his distinct presence at NATO headquarters, which is best illustrated by his green, armored Rolls-Royce, in which he would "majestically tour Brussels." When Luns left his post as secretary general, his successor Lord Peter Carrington's first act was to sell the Rolls-Royce.[59]

After Luns left NATO in 1984, President Ronald Reagan, noting his exceptional and distinguished leadership at NATO, presented him with the highest civilian award in the United States, the Medal of Freedom.[60] Given the Cold War tensions as well as the transatlantic differences during these times, Luns was constrained politically in what he could do to foster alliance consensus during his leadership. Some maintain that Luns occupied the office far beyond the point when he could be an effective secretary general. Although his wit and charisma always remained, he often came to meetings unprepared on the nuances of current defense affairs.[61] At the same time, the fact that there was no movement to remove him from office suggests that the Reagan administration was satisfied with having a secretary general who was sympathetic to its positions but poorly versed at times on the issues of the day.

PETER CARRINGTON, 1984–1988

Lord Peter Carrington became NATO's sixth secretary general on June 25, 1984. Lord Carrington had served previously as the United

58. "Consummate Diplomat Who Believed in Europe," at http://www.rnw.nl/hotspots/html/lunsobit.html.

59. See Shea, "Obituary: Joseph Luns," and, on Carrington, Abshire, *Preventing World War III,* 74.

60. Ronald Reagan, "Toasts of the President and Secretary General Joseph M.A.H. Luns at a Dinner Honoring the NATO Foreign Ministers on the Thirty-fifth Anniversary of the North Atlantic Alliance," *Public Papers of the Presidents,* May 30, 1984, 763–65.

61. Robin Beard, former NATO assistant secretary general, phone interview with author, August 4, 2003. Although he words it carefully, David Abshire implies similar dissatisfaction with Luns's leadership (Abshire, *Preventing World War III,* 67).

Kingdom's defense secretary and foreign secretary. In his memoirs, former U.S. defense secretary Caspar Weinberger notes that Carrington "served with extraordinary skill and effectiveness." David M. Abshire, former U.S. ambassador to NATO, had similar sentiments on Carrington's ability to promote consensus and encourage cooperation. Carrington was a welcome change from Luns and was viewed as an adept manager of the alliance as secretary general.[62]

As is the case with all the previous secretaries general, Lord Carrington never faced a situation in which NATO was called upon to use force, as it was on a number of occasions in the post–Cold War era. Yet, like his predecessors, Carrington was faced with internal political debates and controversies that threatened alliance cohesion. Arguably, Carrington's greatest achievement as secretary general came in his handling of pressures from the U.S. Congress, which in the mid-1980s placed considerable demands on the European allies to increase their defense spending. Led by the efforts of Senator Sam Nunn (D-GA), Congress threatened the removal of some American forces from Europe if the allies did not invest more in their defenses. Abshire notes that in response to this growing transatlantic crisis Carrington was a "genius" in appealing to both Senator Nunn and the Europeans in helping promote greater burden sharing and higher defense spending from the Europeans. In this process, Carrington was critical in drafting NATO communiqués and in assuring NATO's military leaders that its civilian political leaders were all interested in achieving the same end goals.[63]

Lord Carrington is also credited with managing intra-alliance differences over the Reagan administration's proposals for a Strategic Defense Initiative (SDI) and for major missile reductions in Europe at the 1986 U.S.-Soviet Summit at Reykjavik. Both issues generated concern in Europe, and were initially pursued by the United States unilaterally, with limited consultation with the European allies. Abshire even notes that he had been instructed not to talk about the strategic impact of SDI at NATO, and similarly admits that he was unaware of the proposals that were initiated by Reagan officials at Reykjavik. A number of the European foreign and defense ministers

---

62. Caspar Weinberger, *Fighting for Peace: Seven Critical Years in the Pentagon* (New York: Warner Books, 1990), 209; Abshire, *Preventing World War III,* 67; Beard interview, August 4, 2003.
63. Abshire, *Preventing World War III,* 75–76.

were seeking open discussions of how these proposals would affect the alliance and their own security, discussions that the United States resisted at the time. Abshire adds that Carrington again was especially skilled at dampening the intra-alliance differences, and that he "deserved another medal of honor" for helping to find common positions in the alliance.[64] Much evidence suggests that like Secretary General Brosio, Carrington handled internal crises well.

Yet despite the high regard that some have for Carrington, he too was limited in his ability to lead the alliance. One noteworthy example is the Reagan administration's April 14, 1986, decision, made without any consultation in Brussels, to authorize air and naval strikes on Libyan leader Muammar Qaddafi in response to a previous terrorist incident at a German nightclub. Abshire notes in his memoirs that approximately seven hours after the attack, in a specially convened meeting of the NATO ambassadors, Abshire informed his colleagues of the attack. He adds that if the ambassadors "were trying to hold the alliance together, never was there a more dramatic contrast between European and American public attitudes." Abshire recalls that there was "much criticism" directed at the United States. His memoirs include a quote from Carrington, who declared that "the situation is as bad between Europe and America as I can remember in the period I have been associated with the Alliance." Hans van den Broek of the Netherlands, head of the European Community at the time, personally phoned Secretary of State George Shultz to tell him that the strikes "would do serious harm to the transatlantic relationship."[65]

The absence of consultation with NATO is even more extraordinary when one considers that it was NATO's American SACEUR, General Bernard Rogers, who oversaw the bombing operation. Compounding the general European opposition to the air strikes against Libya, France had refused permission for U.S.-based bombers sta-

64. Ibid., 174–78.

65. Ronald Reagan, "Letter to the Speaker of the House of Representatives and the President Pro Tempore of the Senate of the United States on the United States Air Strike against Libya," *Public Papers of the Presidents,* April 16, 1986, 478. See also "Reagan, Officials' Statements on Libya," *Congressional Quarterly Weekly* (April 19, 1986), 881. Abshire, *Preventing World War III,* 85; George P. Shultz, *Turmoil and Triumph: My Years as Secretary of State* (New York: Charles Scribner's Sons, 1993), 687.

tioned in the United Kingdom to use French airspace on their way to Libya. Such actions had caused tremendous anti-French sentiment in the U.S. Congress.[66] As is evident, NATO was a minor player in American foreign policy in this instance. Moreover, as demonstrated earlier, both the SDI and the Reagan administration's arms-control proposals similarly came in the absence of meaningful discussion with the NATO allies. Perhaps this is one reason that Lord Carrington allegedly commented to Manfred Wörner, upon Wörner's installation as NATO's secretary general in 1988, "Now it is up to you to bore yourself for the next four years, Manfred." This quote comports with the feelings of some NATO staff members who served alongside Carrington, who maintain that he "hated being" secretary general.[67]

Overall, Carrington managed intra-alliance disputes adeptly and gracefully. A number of senior Reagan administration officials maintain that he served effectively as secretary general. At the same time, other evidence suggests that Carrington personally recognized the political limitations of being secretary general.[68] Such sentiments are, in part, understandable for the Cold War secretary general. Although agreement exists among analysts that the office was occupied by talented diplomats whose support for transatlantic cooperation was never in question, the evidence seems clear that Cold War secretaries general faced different and difficult leadership hurdles in each case.

Perhaps the most significant constraint on the Cold War secretary general was French president Charles de Gaulle, who had profound impact on the terms of Spaak, Stikker, and Brosio. American unilateralism and independence during the Nixon, Carter, and Reagan administrations at times also relegated NATO to a distant position in international affairs. In this respect, Secretaries General Luns and Carrington also faced tremendous leadership challenges during

66. Dan Smith, *Pressure*, 86.

67. Carrington, quoted in Michael Rühle, "Preface: Manfred Wörner's Legacy and NATO," in *Civil-Military Relations in Post-Communist States: Central and Eastern Europe in Transition*, ed. Anton A. Bebler (Westport, CT: Praeger, 1997), x; senior NATO official "A," correspondence with author, June 15, 2004.

68. Hans Mouritzen, *The International Civil Service: A Study of Bureaucracy: International Organizations* (Aldeshot, England: Dartmouth Publishing Co., 1990), 111.

their tenures. In most cases, too, the secretaries general were over-shadowed by strong SACEURs, especially in the case of Lauris Norstad.

Moreover, during the Cold War, NATO's fundamental mission was vastly different from what it is today. The wider and more "political" role that NATO plays today was almost impossible to imagine during the Cold War and even into the early 1990s, when the alliance struggled to define its new strategic objectives in the Soviet Union's absence. NATO was not asked to use force and provide peacekeeping assistance during the Cold War, and consequently the leadership jurisdiction of the secretaries general was limited and in some cases was purposely restricted—as was done by Manlio Brosio and Joseph Luns. NATO faced many intra-alliance crises and difficult periods in transatlantic relations, and the secretaries general performed admirably if not brilliantly in some cases, but the policy discourse at NATO headquarters never reached the levels witnessed in the post–Cold War era, when NATO became a lead forum for military action in a number of instances. The new security milieu, coupled with the Clinton administration's interest in pursuing foreign policy through the alliance, presented the secretaries general with vastly different leadership roles and opportunities at NATO after the Cold War.

2

Manfred Wörner and the Crisis in Bosnia

As demonstrated in Chapter 1, NATO's secretary general occupied a unique leadership position in world affairs during the Cold War—one that was constrained by a number of political factors. These limitations included strong member-state interests, in many cases a powerful SACEUR, and institutional checks on the secretary general's authority to lead the alliance. With the Soviet Union's collapse and the corresponding political transformation that NATO initiated at its Rome Summit in 1991, however, the alliance was poised to undertake new missions and operations. Ostensibly, one may then expect that NATO's post–Cold War secretary general was faced with new leadership opportunities in this new international environment. And in fact, NATO did adapt in the 1990s, especially in the area of military affairs, with the use of force in Bosnia and Yugoslavia, and later as it faced the crisis with Iraq in 2003. Before beginning the analysis of NATO's post–Cold War secretaries general and their roles in managing the alliance when these issues were considered, some discussion of the analytical approach used in the remainder of the book is merited.

RESEARCH APPROACH AND ANALYTICAL MODEL

NATO's secretary general is challenging to research analytically. Since NATO's principal role revolves around its members' national

39

security interests, press coverage of the organization's decision-making process, and therefore also of the secretary general, is limited. Much of the leadership provided by NATO's secretary general is exercised in closed-door sessions of the North Atlantic Council (NAC) or in informal discussions in NATO's hallways. In addition, the documentary evidence on NATO's NAC discussions requires the approval of all member states before it can be released to the public, which is usually thirty years after an event occurs. Given such limitations, the case-study approach, with reliance upon interviews with senior political and military leaders at NATO, is the most useful method for examining the leadership of a secretary general. Where possible, these interviews have been directly cited and referenced. In a number of interviews, however, senior NATO officials, ambassadors, and others would not permit direct referencing of these conversations. These interviews were granted "on background only" and have been cited with only general reference to the positions held at the time of the events discussed in the interviews.

The post–Cold War cases to be examined include four instances when NATO's secretary general faced the question of use of force. These cases include Manfred Wörner's handling of the crisis in Bosnia, Willy Claes's role during NATO's 1995 bombing of the Bosnian Serbs, Javier Solana's leadership during the seventy-eight-day bombing campaign against Yugoslavia in 1999, and Lord George Robertson's management of NATO as it considered defensive measures for Turkey prior to Operation Iraqi Freedom in 2003. Although the leadership of the secretaries general could be tested across a host of issues, including how they affected NATO's membership expansion, their influence at NATO summits, or their relations with Russia, the decision to use force is arguably different from other issues in that it entails some of the most difficult political and even moral questions for governments. NATO's post–Cold War military actions also represent some of the most vivid examples of the alliance's evolution since the Soviet Union's collapse. NATO never officially engaged in any military action until its strikes on the Bosnian Serbs in 1994. Institutionally, its uses of force were clear illustrations that its role in transatlantic security was fundamentally different from that in its Cold War existence.

Besides the substantive and historical value in focusing on NATO's military actions after the Cold War, there is also analytical value in narrowing the analysis to use-of-force questions involving each secretary general. In doing so, the prospects for more fruitful comparisons grow across these case studies and, arguably, produce better comparative insights on NATO's political leadership.

In examining NATO's secretary general in the post–Cold War era, and with the objective of seeking some comparative value in the cases that follow, Michael G. Schechter's framework for assessing Cold War intergovernmental organization (IGO) leaders offers a useful starting point.[1] When studying the leaders of the World Bank, the United Nations Development Program, and the United Nations Educational, Scientific, and Cultural Organization, Schechter maintained that three aspects of IGO leadership demand close scrutiny: the leader's ability to operate within the systemic political conditions, that is, asking how the leader responds to the wider political environment in which he/she operates; the leader's organization itself, asking what leadership opportunities exist within the organization; and finally, Schechter examined the leader's personality, asking how personal and idiosyncratic qualities affect one's ability to lead. In general, much of Schechter's framework can be useful for assessing NATO's secretary general, although some adaptation of this model may help improve it for the cases that follow.

The influence each post–Cold War secretary general exercised in three "leadership forums" will be examined. First, at the systemic level, the primary factor for analysis will be the secretary general's role in influencing the international political conditions prior to the use of force, as well as how these systemic political conditions may have shaped his ability to lead the alliance. Unlike the constraints placed upon Lord Ismay when he served as secretary general, NATO's secretary general today has wider discretion in how he chooses to address the international political conditions facing the alliance. A secretary general is by definition a representative of all the allies, and has little independent authority apart from his minimal organizational powers at NATO. At the same time, the secretary general may or may not attempt to steer NATO's public political agenda as he desires. The secretary general can do little

1. Michael G. Schechter, "Leadership in International Organizations: Systemic, Organizational and Personality Factors," *Review of International Studies* 13, no. 3 (1987): 197–220.

without support from the NATO allies, but can still choose to be active, passive, or a combination of both when facing the broader international political constraints or opportunities. This leadership forum includes assessments of the relationship the secretaries general may have had with other international organizations, including the United Nations, but mostly focuses upon the broader political factors outside of NATO that may have shaped their leadership options.

At the organizational level, the secretary general's leadership of the North Atlantic Council, NATO's principal decision-making body, provides a second useful avenue for assessing leadership. As was recommended by "the Three Wise Men" in 1956, the secretary general is still charged with overseeing the council through his power to call meetings and set the council's agenda. As during the Cold War, though, the post–Cold War secretary general has no vote within the council, but the council still provides the primary organizational forum for him to exercise some formal (albeit limited) leadership of the alliance. In some cases, in part depending upon the diplomatic skills and political relationships of the secretary general, his leadership role of the NAC can also potentially allow him access to heads of governments—and can be another important aspect of his organizational leadership. One interesting aspect of his organizational power, the use of the "silence procedure" (discussed in Chapters 4 and 5), is another important tool that will also be examined within this framework.

Schechter's third variable, personality, is less useful as a distinct category of analysis for NATO's secretary general. At NATO, the secretary general's personality is often difficult to isolate from his leadership role across all forums. As will be demonstrated, the secretary general's personality and idiosyncratic qualities appear to affect his leadership in all forums, and therefore will not be treated as an independent category of analysis, but rather as a potential political variable across all the forums.

It has become clear in the course of this study that an additional variable is necessary to study the unique position of NATO's secretary general. The final leadership forum to be considered in this analysis is crafted to specifically examine the secretary general's leadership in the realm of civil-military relations. This forum assesses the secretary general's relationship with the SACEUR. Given the SACEUR's previously recognized and historically important role at NATO, especially in the cases of Eisenhower and Norstad, this modification of Schechter's framework is justifiable for examining this unique aspect of political leadership at NATO. Such an approach, in many respects, squares with Robert S. Jordan's study of the first four secretaries general at NATO. Jordan does not create a separate category of analysis for the SACEUR–secretary general relationship, but he does discuss this relationship in each chapter of his book.[2] In addition, this leadership forum is appropriate for the issue under consideration, given that the focus of each case study to follow is NATO's uses of force in the post–Cold War world. This assessment model is summarized in Table 1.

TABLE 1

Leadership Assessment Model for NATO's Secretary General

POTENTIAL LEADERSHIP FORUMS	FACTOR(S) FOR ANALYSIS
Systemic	Contribution in shaping the international political agenda on a given issue, and how the international political system may have shaped his leadership role.
Organizational	Leadership role exercised as chairman of NATO's North Atlantic Council.
Civil-Military Relations	Relationship with the SACEUR, including the role exercised in military planning.

This analytical framework potentially offers a useful guide for assessing the secretaries general, and increases the chances for more fruitful comparisons of NATO's political leaders as they faced use-of-force debates within the alliance.[3]

There are important limitations to this approach. First, the case

2. Robert S. Jordan with Michael W. Bloome, *Political Leadership in NATO: A Study in Multinational Diplomacy* (Boulder, CO: Westview Press, 1979).

3. For more on case study research and the prospects for generalization, see Robert Yin, *Case Study Research: Design and Methods,* 2nd ed. (Thousand Oaks, CA: Sage Publications, 1994).

studies considered in this book are not comprehensive assessments of each secretary general's leadership tenure. The secretaries general clearly exercised leadership across other issues faced by the alliance, which are not necessarily focused upon or examined in these cases. Moreover, each secretary general faced different use-of-force considerations; the cases are clearly not perfectly analogous. The analytical framework employed here, however, allows for these considerations to be addressed to some degree.

If the secretary general had already established a leadership "legacy" on other issues at NATO that may have affected his wider ability to influence NATO decisions on the use of force, these leadership factors will be considered within the framework. As became clear in a number of interviews, Manfred Wörner's and Javier Solana's previous leadership roles on other issues shaped their ability to lead the alliance when military action was considered. In these cases, an attempt has been made to recognize other critical moments in a secretary general's tenure that may have been relevant when force was considered by the alliance.

In addition, while each case considered is somewhat different from the others in terms of the political conditions faced by the alliance and the kind of military action that NATO employed, the reliance upon this revised version of Schechter's model allows for these different systemic conditions to be discussed and factored into the analysis. Moreover, such a limited study of specific cases of *military* action allows for more structured, focused case studies, which increases the chances for more generalizable findings.[4]

In the case studies that follow, it will become evident that the personalities and diplomatic approaches of the secretaries general varied considerably. Manfred Wörner, who led the alliance when it first faced the crisis in Bosnia, remains deeply revered at NATO headquarters today, in large part due to his personal leadership and perseverance on Bosnia. This crisis in the Balkans in the early and mid-1990s presented NATO with a question of legitimacy. In its post–Cold War transformation, NATO faced an "out-of-area" conflict that threatened stability across southern Europe and became a humanitarian tragedy of the sort that Europe had not experienced

4. Alexander L. George, "Case Studies and Theory Development: The Method of Structured, Focused Comparison," in *Diplomacy: New Approaches in History, Theory, and Policy,* ed. Paul Gordon Lauren (New York: Free Press, 1979), 43–68.

since the Second World War. On August 30, 1995, NATO responded with a bombing campaign that lasted nearly two weeks, eventually resulting in the Dayton Peace Accords and, later, stability in Bosnia. While NATO's eventual military response to the crisis assisted in the preservation of the alliance and helped to fundamentally reshape its post–Cold War mission, the problems in Bosnia generated profound and divisive debates within NATO, and presented its first post–Cold War secretary general, Manfred Wörner, with enormous political challenges.

MANFRED WÖRNER, 1988–1994

Manfred Wörner became NATO's seventh secretary general on July 1, 1988, when he replaced Lord Peter Carrington, who had served in the position since 1984. Wörner came to NATO with exceptional military and defense credentials. In the six years before his appointment, he served as West Germany's defense minister. Prior to this position, in 1965 he was elected to serve in the German Bundestag, and for many of the following years served as a leading voice for Germany's Christian Democratic Union (CDU) on defense issues, culminating in his chairmanship of the Bundestag's Defense Committee and vice chairmanship of the CDU. Before his entry into politics, Wörner had earned a doctorate in international law, specializing in military issues.

Wörner's selection as secretary general came with considerable controversy, primarily between Germany and Norway. Upon Carrington's retirement announcement in 1987, Norway recommended its former prime minister, Kaare Willoch, as his replacement. Chancellor Helmut Kohl of Germany responded to Willoch's candidacy by announcing his support for Manfred Wörner. As Germany's defense minister, Wörner had been a strong advocate of President Ronald Reagan's Cold War policies, including the Strategic Defense Initiative (SDI), American missile deployments to Europe, and continued calls for high defense spending. This advocacy made him less appealing to some Europeans. If selected as secretary general, Wörner would also be the first German to lead the alliance. With these two candidates in contention for NATO's leadership post, debate continued for months among the allies, with the Norwegians and Germans remaining firmly committed to their "nominees." Eventually, however, with full and openly expressed backing from the United States, Wörner emerged as the clear favorite and Willoch withdrew his candidacy.[5]

Wörner became NATO's political leader just as the Soviet Union began to collapse and as monumental strategic changes occurred across Europe. Although the focus of this chapter is Wörner's leadership on Bosnia, it is noteworthy that in his first years as secretary general, he is credited by many ambassadors and analysts as being crucial in pushing NATO to transform itself as the Soviet Union collapsed. Many see Wörner as forward looking in his belief that NATO should reach out to Russia and the newly created democracies of Eastern Europe to create new partnerships. What is evident is that on an array of issues facing NATO, even during his first weeks as secretary general, Wörner pushed forward his own views, sometimes quite vigorously, on what was best for the alliance.[6] As will be demonstrated in the chapters to follow, Wörner was unique in this regard among the post–Cold War secretaries general; he did not shy away from taking controversial positions long before consensus among the allies had been reached. Although he did not always succeed, it is apparent that he viewed his office as an independent force for action within the alliance. This degree of activism was clear regarding Yugoslavia when it erupted into civil war.

Systemic Conditions Facing Wörner

The wars in Yugoslavia began in the summer of 1991, when Slovenia broke away from the Federal Republic of Yugoslavia and gained its independence in its "ten-day war." These events trig-

5. James M. Markham, "Oslo and Bonn at Odds on New NATO Chief," *New York Times*, November 25, 1987, A11; Serge Schmemann, "Norwegian Withdraws, Enabling German to Hold Top NATO Post," *New York Times*, December 1, 1987, A8.

6. Dan Oberdorfer, "New NATO Head Cautiously Optimistic," *Washington Post*, September 14, 1988, A18; Robert Hunter, former U.S. ambassador to NATO, phone interview with author, July 7, 2003; Lambert Willem Veenendaal, former Netherlands ambassador to NATO, phone interview with author, July 23, 2003; Daniel Christman, former U.S. military representative to NATO, phone interview with author, July 8, 2003; Thorstein Ingolfsson, Iceland ambassador to NATO, phone interview with author, September 2, 2003.

gered a Croatian independence movement, which was followed closely by secessionist claims by Bosnia and Herzegovina and Croatia in 1992. From 1992 to 1995, Croatia and nearly all of Bosnia remained engulfed in conflict, as Yugoslavian president Slobodan Milosevic actively supported Bosnian Serb factions who operated across the region. In 1992 and 1993, reports surfaced that the Balkans were experiencing atrocities at levels that Europe had not seen since the Second World War: prisoner-of-war camps, civilian deaths, rapes, and other widespread human-rights violations sparked memories of what had been done to the Jews in Nazi Germany.[7]

From the time the Balkans turned violent until his death on August 13, 1994, while still in office, Wörner faced an alliance that was deeply torn over how to handle the crisis. In 1992 and throughout much of 1993, NATO's most powerful members preferred limited intervention in the region. Most importantly, President George H. W. Bush of the United States and his administration favored little more than United Nations–sponsored humanitarian assistance and viewed the problem and solutions as essentially "European." Secretary of State James Baker allegedly maintained inside the Bush administration that the United States did not "have a dog in this fight."[8]

Although Arkansas governor Bill Clinton criticized Bush's handling of the Bosnia crisis during the 1992 presidential campaign and called for a more assertive American military presence, once elected president he too resisted sustained military intervention in 1993 and 1994.[9] Although some senior foreign policy makers, most notably Clinton's national security advisor, Anthony Lake, were encouraging more aggressive policy approaches and occasionally succeeded in

7. Ivo H. Daalder, *Getting to Dayton: The Making of America's Bosnia Policy* (Washington, DC: Brookings Institution Press, 2000), 18; Gale Stokes, *Three Eras of Political Change in Eastern Europe* (New York: Oxford University Press, 1997); Michael A. Sells, *The Bridge Betrayed* (Berkeley: University of California Press, 1996); Christopher Bennett, *Yugoslavia's Bloody Collapse: Causes, Course and Consequences* (New York: New York University Press, 1995).

8. James A. Baker III with Thomas M. DeFrank, *The Politics of Diplomacy* (New York: Putnam, 1995), 651; Baker, quoted in Richard Holbrooke, *To End a War* (New York: Random House, 1998), 27.

9. Barton Gellman, "U.S. Military Fears Balkan Intervention," *New York Times,* August 12, 1992, A24; Ronald D. Asmus, *Opening NATO's Door: How the Alliance Remade Itself for a New Era* (New York: Columbia University Press, 2003), 21.

producing small policy shifts toward military options, many ac-
counts of the Clinton administration indicate that the White House
was focused mostly on domestic political issues, which changed
only with the crisis in Somalia in October 1993.[10] In May 1993, when
the Clinton administration initially began to address Bosnia through
diplomatic means among the allies, Secretary of State Warren Christopher went to Brussels for a NATO meeting, and European leaders
were surprised to find that he was not offering an American leadership role, but rather came to Europe in a consultative and "conciliatory" manner.[11] Christopher's approach demonstrated that the United
States was really not ready to take the lead on Bosnia, and that the
Clinton administration remained as confused as all others on how
best to address the conflict. Given the United States' tremendous
political influence within NATO, the Clinton administration's absence of leadership on Bosnia is an important systemic factor that
Wörner faced.

Another systemic influence for Wörner was the heightened role
of the United Nations in international relations in the early 1990s.
Initially, the European Community had attempted to play a conflict-
resolution role on Yugoslavia. A memorable quote from Foreign
Minister Jacques Poos of Luxembourg, that the problem in the Balkans represented "the hour of Europe," however, proved to be mostly
rhetoric. Political differences among the Europeans, as well as Europe's recognition that it would need broader assistance to face the
profound problems in the Balkans, shifted diplomatic initiatives to
the United Nations in July 1992.[12] Moreover, with the coalition forces'
Desert Storm victory over Iraq in 1991 and the Soviet Union's col-

10. David Halberstam, *War in a Time of Peace: Bush, Clinton and the Generals*
(New York: Scribner, 2001); Douglas C. Foyle, "Public Opinion and Bosnia:
Anticipating Disaster," in *Contemporary Cases in U.S. Foreign Policy*, ed. Ralph
G. Carter (Washington, DC: Congressional Quarterly Press, 2002), 32–58.

11. Christopher himself described his approach as "conciliatory" (Daalder,
Getting to Dayton, 15–17).

12. Poos, quoted in Stanley R. Sloan, *NATO, the European Union, and the
Atlantic Community* (Lanham, MD: Rowman and Littlefield, 2003), 94; James B.
Steinberg, "International Involvement in the Yugoslavia Conflict," in *Enforcing
Restraint: Collective Intervention in Internal Conflicts*, ed. Lori Fisler Damrosch
(New York: Council on Foreign Relations, 1993), 36–46; Jane Boulden, *Peace
Enforcement: The United Nations Experience in Congo, Somalia, and Bosnia*
(Westport, CT: Praeger, 2001), 85.

lapse, newfound optimism about a "new world order" and stronger support for the United Nations existed in many governments.

When the crisis broke out, the UN Security Council imposed sanctions, most notably a weapons embargo, on Yugoslavia. On February 21, 1992, it also endorsed a peacekeeping force, the United Nations Protection Force (UNPROFOR), which was intended to produce a calming effect in Croatia and Bosnia so that the diplomatic efforts under way would have a greater chance of success. Over the course of 1992, 1993, and 1994, however, diplomacy continued to fail as the Bosnian Serbs made a mockery of the United Nations' presence in the region. By November 30, 1994, more than thirty-eight thousand UNPROFOR soldiers were stationed across Bosnia and Croatia, including soldiers from Belgium, Canada, Denmark, France, the Netherlands, Norway, Spain, and the United Kingdom—all NATO members.[13] Many of the UN troops were attempting to protect specific cities or "enclaves" where the United Nations called for a complete cessation of armed conflict and attempted to deliver humanitarian assistance. These enclaves proved to be anything but safe. Yet despite the failing operation, the United Nations remained the diplomatic hub for policy decisions on the Balkans.

Besides the growing political and diplomatic role for the United Nations in world politics, it also gained an operational role on the ground with UNPROFOR, which had another important effect on NATO's political independence. On August 3, 1993, NATO agreed to a "dual-key" arrangement with the United Nations. With UNPROFOR troops increasingly under fire while attempting to deliver humanitarian assistance and shelter to thousands of civilians in need, NATO and UN officials agreed to a joint decision-making process for approving military action to protect these troops: before NATO could use force in response to a provocation on UNPROFOR, UN and NATO officials would have to concur that a military response was warranted; both would have to turn their metaphorical "keys."

While many NATO members favored continued UN involve-

13. The number of soldiers not including police or other observers from each of these countries on November 30, 1994, was: Belgium, 1,038; Canada, 2,091; Denmark, 1,230; France, 4,493; the Netherlands, 1,803; Norway, 826; Spain, 1,212; and the United Kingdom, 3,405. See the UN web site at http://www.un.org/Depts/dpko/dpko/co_mission/unprofor.htm.

ment, the British and French were especially insistent that a role for the United Nations remain preserved and that NATO be limited in its participation in Bosnia at the time. Within NATO, Canada was also especially adamant that NATO's operational authority be controlled by the United Nations. There was a fear that without the United Nations' "checking" role, a military operation could quickly become "Americanized," so the preference remained among the Europeans and especially Canada for a strong UN role, which the United States grudgingly accepted as the only compromise possible.[14]

In the case of the United Nations' "key," it was in the hands of the UN secretary general's special representative, Yasushi Akashi, who often received advice and oversight from the UN secretary general, Boutros Boutros-Ghali. At NATO, the key was held by the commander in chief of Allied Forces Southern Europe, who in August 1993 was Admiral Jeremy M. Boorda of the United States. Boorda's successor, Admiral Leighton W. Smith, also of the United States, similarly held NATO's key at the time of Operation Deliberate Force in August 1995. In this regard, the UN civilian leadership held veto power over NATO military commanders, which translated into profound limitations on Wörner's ability to influence the broader international environment and on NATO's ability to act.[15]

Another systemic effect that resulted from UNPROFOR's presence was a political divide among the Europeans about how to proceed militarily. Many European countries, as well as Canada, understood the problems and limits of UNPROFOR's peacekeeping efforts, but feared that use-of-force options would place their peacekeeping forces at risk of retribution from the warring factions. Thus, until Wörner's death, NATO's role in Bosnia remained secondary to the UN peacekeeping mission, despite its failings.

Two additional systemic factors, however, arguably worked in favor of NATO engagement. The first was that Russia consistently

14. In his memoirs, James K. Bartleman, former Canadian ambassador to NATO, takes credit for demanding the dual-key framework (Bartleman, *On Six Continents: A Life in Canada's Foreign Service* [Toronto: McClelland and Stewart, 2004], 213). Col. Robert C. Owen, "Summary," in *Deliberate Force: A Case Study in Effective Air Campaigning,* ed. Col. Robert C. Owen (Maxwell Air Force Base, AL: Air University Press, 2000), 473.

15. Ivo H. Daalder, *Getting to Dayton,* 22–23; Lt. Col. Ronald M. Reed, "Chariots of Fire: Rules of Engagement in Operation Deliberate Force," in *Deliberate Force: A Case Study in Effective Air Campaigning,* 402–3.

and vehemently opposed more aggressive use-of-force options at the UN Security Council. Russia was not alone in expressing such caution, and by early 1994 some transatlantic momentum for policy change was evident, which encouraged a tentative shift of diplomatic venues from the United Nations to NATO, where Russia's UN Security Council veto power was moot.[16]

The other systemic influence that potentially favored a role for NATO was its transformed strategic doctrine, which had first been recommended at the London Summit in 1990 and was codified at the Rome Summit in November 1991. In Rome, NATO announced that it could undertake non–Article 5 operations, which included future roles in conflict resolution, crisis prevention, and peacekeeping. Although it reiterated that NATO's primary mission remained the defense of its member states, the new Strategic Concept indicated that NATO was evolving toward something markedly different from its Cold War identity.[17] But as the United Nations remained the political and diplomatic center of action, the worsening crisis in the Balkans increasingly became viewed as a test of whether NATO could address this post–Cold War challenge in Europe, and of whether NATO could adapt to its newly stated missions. In this respect, the United Nations' miserable performance in Bosnia increasingly shifted the world's attention to NATO and whether it could surmount this new challenge.

In sum, the systemic political conditions from 1991 to 1994 placed immense political obstacles in Wörner's path. On Bosnia, he most often faced a cautious and hesitant alliance. For much of this period, NATO's de facto leader, the United States, was unwilling to exercise leadership. When the United States attempted to steer the alliance toward more aggressive policy decisions, as it did in August 1993, most Europeans favored the United Nations' "check" on American military power from NATO. The European allies resisted an aggressive role for NATO because of the potential risk to their troops on the ground in UNPROFOR. Moreover, most of the substantive policy decisions occurred at the UN Security Council—not at NATO. Russian opposition in the Security Council to military strikes and talk of NATO's growing "credibility crisis" created some interest in

16. Boulden, *Peace Enforcement*, 95.
17. "The Alliance's New Strategic Concept," November 7–8, 1991, NATO, http://www.nato.int/docu/comm/49-95/c911107a.htm.

using NATO to resolve the conflict, but most of the systemic factors worked against NATO engagement during Wörner's tenure.

When, under similar circumstances, NATO's secretaries general have faced acute policy differences among the allies, nearly all have refrained from seeking major policy changes. As established in Chapter 1, successful independent policy entrepreneurship is not the legacy of NATO's political leadership. The only previous secretary general who attempted to lead from the front, Paul-Henri Spaak, was isolated politically when he attempted to steer the alliance in new directions.[18] Yet, despite Spaak's failures and the traditional practice for secretaries general under similar political conditions, Wörner challenged the norm and openly strove for vigorous and active NATO engagement in Bosnia.

In a number of major public addresses in 1993, Wörner made clear his view that NATO should take a more active stance toward stopping the atrocities in Bosnia. In facing the systemic constraints, Wörner focused most of his attention on encouraging American leadership of NATO and on the United Nations' inability to resolve the conflict. Many of his public addresses in 1993 called forcefully for NATO action, despite the deep divisions in the alliance at the time. Wörner wanted NATO to accept new roles in security after the Cold War and simultaneously argued that the United Nations did not have the organizational resources necessary to address Bosnia's problems. In May 1993, before NATO had taken a major policy decision on Bosnia, with the Clinton administration wavering over what to do, Wörner pushed for NATO intervention. In an implicit critique aimed at all NATO capitals and, more generally, the United Nations, he noted, "We all wish that diplomatic means alone would succeed. But diplomacy needs to be backed up with a determination to use force if it is to be credible. . . . As Frederick the Great used to say: 'Diplomacy without the sword is like music without instruments.'" In the same speech, on the growing crisis in Yugoslavia and the United Nations' actions there, he added, "In short: you need NATO. The United Nations are overstretched and underfunded."[19]

18. Jordan, *Political Leadership in NATO*, 71–75.

19. Manfred Wörner, "Speech by the Secretary General at the Centro Alti Study Difese, Rome, May 10, 1993," NATO, http://www.nato.int/docu/speech/1993/s93051a.htm.

As the weeks progressed in 1993, and as American policy toward Bosnia floated without direction, Wörner's tacit criticism of the United States grew less tacit. Wörner was a strong advocate of American leadership of NATO; he viewed U.S. support as critical in determining NATO's relevance in the world. His belief in America's military capabilities and its natural leadership role stemmed from the dominant military presence of the United States within the alliance, but also from a deeper historical and personal connection to the United States. His colleagues note that Wörner often recounted his experience as a German boy, watching when American tanks rolled into Germany to liberate the country from the Nazi regime. Wörner could recall vividly from his youth the American soldiers in Germany who handed him sticks of gum during the U.S. occupation. His disappointment with the United States and the Clinton administration's leadership vacuum on Bosnia was grounded not only in what he felt was needed at NATO, but also in his genuine personal belief in what he believed was the appropriate role for the United States in transatlantic security. His disappointment was evident to many—both publicly and privately.[20]

In a speech in September 1993, only a month after the dual-key decision was codified, Wörner argued openly for military action in the Balkans. In a critique of the dominant American military thought at the time, which was best articulated through the "Powell Doctrine," named after Colin Powell, then the chairman of the Joint Chiefs of Staff, that military force should only be used overwhelmingly and when national security threats were clearly at stake, Wörner maintained that "the purpose of intervention is not necessarily to win a war, but to influence the behaviour of the party concerned. We need to have limited military options for limited political and military objectives. It is wrong to think only in categories of all or nothing."[21]

When he traveled to the United States in October 1993 to make an

---

20. Robin Beard, former NATO assistant secretary general, phone interview with author, August 4, 2003; George Joulwan, former SACEUR, phone interview with author, October 27, 2003; James K. Bartleman, former Canadian ambassador to NATO, phone interview with author, August 8, 2003; Christman interview, July 8, 2003.

21. Manfred Wörner, "Speech by the Secretary General of NATO Mr. Manfred Wörner to the IISS in Brussels, September 10, 1993," NATO, http://www.nato.int/docu/speech/1993/s930910a.htm.

address to the National Press Club, Wörner minced no words about
his preferred role for American leadership in the alliance: "A superpower simply cannot take a sabbatical from history, not even a va-
cation. We need United States' leadership. Without the leadership
of the US there will be no leadership at all, and most likely no meaningful action in crisis situations. Either you meet crises head-on, or
they will jump you from behind."[22]

At NATO headquarters, Wörner did what he could to change the
broader systemic attitudes toward Bosnia in 1993. From the beginning of the crisis, Wörner was supportive of NATO intervention. In
the words of James K. Bartleman, former Canadian ambassador to
NATO, even in 1992 Wörner "believed passionately that NATO had
a moral obligation to help." In addition, when American secretary
of state Warren Christopher traveled to Brussels for a NATO meeting in May 1993, Wörner confided to him that if the United States
asked the alliance to place more pressure on the Bosnian Serbs by
lifting the then imposed arms embargo and threatening military
strikes, for example, the "lift and strike option," Wörner offered to
second such a motion for action. Given that Wörner had already established himself as a forceful and influential secretary general, his
backing would arguably have been quite helpful in moving the
alliance in a new direction. As noted earlier, Christopher refused,
preferring more consultation among the allies.[23] While Wörner
publicly remained on good political terms with the Clinton administration, privately his frustration and disappointment with Secretary Christopher and the American White House was obvious to
many in Brussels.[24]

Wörner's desired policy ends for Bosnia in 1993 and 1994 were
never truly achieved before his death in office in August 1994; not
until August 1995 did NATO undertake vigorous military action
against the Bosnian Serbs. In 1993 and 1994, most of the critical policy decisions remained at the UN Security Council. Under such political constraints, Wörner fought to garner support for NATO's

22. Manfred Wörner, "Speech by Secretary General of NATO Mr. Manfred
Wörner at the National Press Club, October 6, 1993," NATO, http://www.
nato.int/docu/speech/1993/s931006a.htm.

23. Bartleman, On Six Continents, 208; Daalder, Getting to Dayton, 16n38; senior NATO official "A," phone interview with author, September 9, 2003.

24. Beard interview, August 4, 2003.

relevance in Bosnia at this time. Russian opposition helped to shift some policy-making decisions to NATO in February and April 1994, but the dominant systemic conditions, including tentative American leadership and differences among the European allies over how to handle the crisis, limited how much NATO did at this time and Wörner's ability to influence policy in the short term. Despite the adoption of its new Strategic Concept, which ostensibly allowed for the sort of military missions that Wörner sought for Bosnia, the allies generally resisted NATO intervention. In this respect, Wörner's independent influence and ability to shape NATO's broader agenda on Bosnia, despite his impassioned efforts, were limited. The various systemic constraints were simply too great.

At the same time, nearly all decision makers present in Brussels in 1993 and 1994 maintain that Wörner played some role in moving the alliance toward military action. While he did not independently succeed in reshaping NATO's agenda prior to his death, his moral passion and determination to protect NATO's credibility should not be underestimated. He desperately wanted American leadership, a desire that began to surface publicly, albeit in a limited way, in 1993. When the Clinton administration moved to play a greater leadership role on Bosnia, which occurred incrementally beginning in August 1993, the United States had Wörner's personal support, which would be important in the diplomacy that would take place in NATO's corridors. In this respect, Wörner served as an advocate for the American position, when it was voiced, that NATO must take a stronger stand against the Bosnian Serbs' aggression. His public support for NATO intervention and the moral passion that he brought to the issue helped build momentum for the military action that came later, in August 1995.[25]

It is also noteworthy that a secretary general could openly challenge the United States to assume a greater leadership role on Bosnia within the alliance, and yet not become ostracized politically from the Clinton administration in doing so. Such independence is rarely witnessed at NATO; a secretary general runs the risk of alienating the most powerful and important state in the alliance if he

25. Reginald Bartholomew, former U.S. ambassador to NATO, phone interview with author, November 12, 2003; Hunter interview, July 7, 2003; Christman interview, July 8, 2003.

confronts the United States too aggressively. Wörner never severed his excellent diplomatic ties with the Clinton administration, but his willingness to assert such forceful views on Bosnia absent American support is striking, and it goes without comparison in the alliance's history.

In sum, many at NATO viewed Wörner as a forceful and effective leader—even though he was unable to produce the military engagement he desired. The systemic constraints that he operated against were too great, but at the same time should not detract from the cumulative impact of his speeches on NATO's threatened credibility and the atrocities taking place in Bosnia. His leadership in the North Atlantic Council (NAC), where his personal diplomatic strengths could be more fully realized in 1994, is a better indicator of his influence in the alliance.

Organizational Leadership

Before moving specifically to Wörner's leadership in the NAC on Bosnia in 1994, it must first be noted that he became NATO's leader in a time of transition. Not only was the world's political landscape being transformed with the Soviet Union's collapse, so too was the organizational culture of the alliance being transformed. During the Cold War, NATO rarely exhibited a sense of policy urgency. Day-to-day operations were generally routine: meetings that went late into the evening were the exception. Although NATO was hesitant to put its new Strategic Concept into practice, under Wörner's leadership, the work environment at NATO changed considerably. Wörner brought with him much energy and a work ethic that NATO had previously not experienced and that, in effect, changed the organizational culture.[26]

In NAC sessions during Wörner's leadership, and specifically those meetings that addressed Bosnia, Wörner was known for respecting all ambassadors' views. Comments made in multiple interviews suggest that he conducted himself in a very statesmanlike manner, even when he disagreed adamantly with those opposing

26. For a discussion of the organizational political culture of NATO in the 1970s, see Bartleman, *On Six Continents*, 79.

his preferred positions. James K. Bartleman notes that even though he knew Wörner disagreed with the Canadian government's hesitance to use force in Bosnia, Wörner still treated him professionally and respectfully, even when tensions ran high in the alliance.[27]

At the same time, Wörner is also recalled as a secretary general who kept the alliance focused on Bosnia. When ambassadors digressed from the central question or when their remarks became redundant or unhelpful in Wörner's view, the secretary general would interrupt them and redirect the discussion, or ask other ambassadors for their positions.[28] Wörner pushed the ambassadors to avoid discussions of the minutiae and despised debates over the semantical nuances of policy. Occasionally, Wörner would exercise his powers as secretary general in the NAC quite forcefully, and would unabashedly advance his own more "hawkish" views on the question of Bosnia. His "booming" voice and forceful presence in NAC meetings are recalled by many who witnessed him lead. Wörner was fluent in English, French, and German, and he was able to use all three languages while speaking to different ambassadors in the council, which was deemed to be a helpful diplomatic asset in his leadership role. His passion on Bosnia was evident in whatever language he spoke. At the ambassadors' private Tuesday luncheons, he would even more freely advocate his own views that the alliance must go out of area if it wished to remain relevant in its new missions.[29]

Another element of Wörner's effectiveness in the NAC was the fact that he had many diplomatic and personal friendships in politics that he had developed over the years. When ambassadors resisted the policy stands that he sought, he would occasionally threaten to "go above" them and personally appeal to their home

27. Hunter interview, July 7, 2003; Beard interview, August 4, 2003; Bartleman interview, August 8, 2003.

28. Hunter interview, July 7, 2003; Veenendaal interview, July 23, 2003.

29. Beard interview, August 4, 2003; senior U.S. Department of Defense official "A," phone interview with author, September 17, 2003; Robert George, former Canadian military representative to NATO, phone interview with author, July 23, 2003; Christman interview, July 8, 2003; Hunter interview, July 7, 2003; senior NATO official "A," phone interview with author, September 23, 2003; senior U.S. Department of Defense official "B," phone interview with author, July 31, 2003; Veenendaal interview, July 23, 2003; Bartholomew interview, November 12, 2003.

governments for policy change. Wörner's threats had legitimacy because of his well-known passion on Bosnia, but also because his personal list of international contacts ran deep from his many years in German politics. As secretary general, Wörner was a frequent visitor to all member states of the alliance, especially the United States, and thus he continued to cultivate relationships that he had developed in previous years.[30]

As with his efforts to shape NATO's broader agenda in light of the systemic constraints, identifying specific policy changes in the NAC that came about because of Wörner's actions is again difficult. It is important to remember that the secretary general has no vote in the NAC, and always serves at the pleasure of its members. Due to such organizational constraints, political and institutional limitations always exist on what the secretary general can achieve by himself. At the same time, Robert Hunter, former U.S. ambassador to NATO, and Robin Beard, former NATO assistant secretary general, both contend that nothing was going to happen in the NAC without Wörner's approval. Such statements contrast markedly with the history of NATO's Cold War secretaries general, who were often viewed as subordinate to the SACEUR, or who simply did not have the political stature to lead the alliance. The allies saw Wörner as a respected leader whose voice had real political influence and weight. Thus, in the broadest sense, many felt that Wörner's presence and leadership always had an impact in NAC sessions.[31] One occasion of Wörner's leadership in the NAC, however, stands out.

During his last two years as secretary general, Wörner was often absent from NATO headquarters due to his physical trials with cancer and the subsequent medical treatments he received from his primary hospital in Aaken, Germany. During Wörner's periods of sickness and absence from NATO, Italian Sergio Balanzino, NATO's deputy secretary general, presided over NAC meetings—although Wörner always remained informed and very much engaged in NATO business. Even during his most difficult days and up until his last

30. Beard interview, August 4, 2003; Bartholomew interview, November 12, 2003; senior U.S. Department of Defense official "B" interview, July 31, 2003; senior NATO official "A" interview, September 9, 2003.

31. Hunter interview, July 7, 2003; Beard interview, August 4, 2003. Similar points were made by Christman (interview, July 8, 2003) and Veenendaal (interview, July 23, 2003).

days alive, Wörner, from his hospital room, remained immersed in all elements of NATO policy, particularly Bosnia.[32]

While Wörner was hospitalized in April 1994, NATO was considering the expansion of military "exclusion" zones in Bosnia. The Bosnian Serbs had become especially bold in their attacks on UN peacekeepers in the weeks preceding this meeting, and NATO was considering a broader military role in the region. Serb forces had launched a series of attacks on Goradze, an area of Bosnia that had been declared one of the United Nations' "safe havens."[33]

With the NAC stalemated over the developments surrounding Goradze, Wörner, against his physician's advice, rose from his sickbed, removed the intravenous support he was receiving, and had himself driven to Brussels to attend the deadlocked NAC meeting. His physician traveled with him and sat behind him during the session. When interviewed, nearly all key participants who witnessed his presence at this meeting on April 22, 1994, recalled Wörner's leadership vividly. Although Wörner's physical weight had seriously decreased because of his cancer and his treatments, his passion for NATO intervention and his courage to attend the meeting at that time went unmatched. A number of participants clearly remember the intravenous feeding tubes that remained visible near Wörner's shirt collar during the meeting. Certainly, the tragic events on the ground in April 1994 aided his argument that NATO must accept a broader military role against the Bosnian Serbs, but most participants point to Wörner's presence at this meeting as a key factor and in some cases even the critical variable in moving NATO toward military engagement. All participants understood that Wörner personalized the conflict in Bosnia, in that he felt that such horrific events in Bosnia should not be happening on "his watch" as secretary general. The tragedy in Bosnia was not the sort of Europe that he had foreseen in the Soviet Union's absence, and it provided him with tremendous personal motivation for action. From his Aaken hospital room, as he watched on television the Bosnian Serb military attacks against Bosnian hospitals, Wörner felt that he could

---

32. Hunter interview, July 7, 2003; George Joulwan, interview with author, August 27, 2003; George interview, July 23, 2003; senior NATO official "A" interview, September 23, 2003.

33. Daalder, *Getting to Dayton*, 28.

relate personally to the crisis, which heightened his interest in curtailing the Serbs' assaults.[34] As the meeting moved late into the evening on April 22, with Wörner still present, the NAC agreed to a much wider military role in protecting UN safe havens through air power, and Goradze specifically.

Without American support, NATO would not have adopted the extended no-fly zones. Moreover, extensive Bosnian Serb violations of UN mandates, and their willingness to challenge the Western powers and NATO's legitimacy, provided additional incentives for NATO intervention. Yet officials in multiple interviews indicate that Wörner's presence still appears to have been critical in moving the NAC to expand the no-fly zones.

While Wörner's presence at this NAC meeting is recalled by all the participants, there was almost no media coverage through leaks to journalists devoted to his role at this particular session. Part of the reason for the dearth of journalistic attention was Wörner's personally good relationship with the European media and the respect that they had for him. On one occasion, Wörner recorded and broadcasted a public NATO statement from his Aaken hospital room, which was temporarily converted to look like a press briefing room at NATO headquarters. The media respected him, and journalists only rarely made mention of the physical toll that cancer was taking on him. Wörner always felt that he could defeat his cancer, and he despised the appearance of weakness, which meant both his own physical limitations and, more generally, NATO's inability to act.[35] His appearance at this April 1994 NAC meeting is regarded by many as his greatest single leadership act while at NATO, and it demonstrates the organizational influence he could exercise once issues reached the NAC.

Working with the SACEUR: Wörner and George Joulwan

In 1994, when NATO used force in Bosnia under Wörner's leadership, General George Joulwan was serving as SACEUR. Joulwan

---

34. Beard interview, August 4, 2003; senior U.S. Department of Defense official "B," phone interview with author, July 31, 2003; senior NATO official "A" interview, September 23, 2003; Christman interview, July 8, 2003; Joulwan interview, October 27, 2003.

35. Senior NATO official "A" interview, September 23, 2003.

had been appointed SACEUR on October 22, 1993, and came to NATO with a reputation of having a strong and forceful personality.[36] Wörner's relationship with Joulwan is a critically important component of leadership for the secretary general, especially considering that NATO's strikes in Bosnia were the first military strikes ever conducted by the alliance.

Much evidence exists that, during Wörner's leadership, he was actively engaged in all military and defense aspects of NATO. Given his background as Germany's defense minister and his wide knowledge of defense affairs, Wörner had little hesitation in approaching military representatives of NATO's member states, whom he would lobby for higher defense budgets, and he would chastise those who were not investing enough in their military. While Wörner always remained statesmanlike in his interaction with military officials, he was not afraid to approach (and nearly reprimand) them when he wanted change in member states' defense postures.[37]

Prior to Wörner's death, NATO used force in Bosnia on two occasions. One strike, on February 28, 1994, entailed the downing of four Serbian Galeb aircraft that were in violation of the no-fly zones imposed over certain sections of Bosnia, which NATO was authorized to enforce. On April 10 and 11, 1994, NATO forces again struck Bosnian Serb targets, including a small command post consisting of a few vehicles and tents. Wörner was not involved in the target selection or actual military decision-making processes of either of these bombings. The strikes against the Bosnian Serb aircraft happened very quickly and fell directly under NATO's authority to enforce the no-fly zones. NATO's April strikes were directed by the commander of UNPROFOR-Bosnia, General Michael Rose, because of the UN and NATO's joint presence, and involved no specific directions or input from the secretary general.[38]

In terms of developing operational plans for carrying out NATO's military mandates on Bosnia, Wörner allowed SACEUR Joulwan discretion in doing what he felt was necessary. In this respect, Wörner did not try to micromanage NATO's military arm; he granted the SACEUR operational leeway. At the same time, this discretion

---

36. See especially George Graham and Jurek Martin, "Joulwan Named to Head NATO Forces," *Financial Times*, October 5, 1993, 7.

37. George interview, July 23, 2003.

38. Joulwan interview, October 27, 2003.

should not been seen to imply that Wörner allowed Joulwan to operate without his oversight. The secretary general had extensive and detailed knowledge of the operational plans during his entire leadership period. Wörner wanted to be consulted on all aspects of NATO, including military planning, even during his periods of hospitalization. Prior to the dramatic April 22, 1994, NAC meeting, Joulwan traveled to Aaken to consult with Wörner on extending the no-fly zones in the UN safe havens in Bosnia. When Wörner felt that NATO was not being aggressive enough in enforcing NAC decisions, he would personally phone Joulwan and express his frustration. Such phone calls would be made from Brussels, as well as from Wörner's hospital room.[39]

Much of Wörner's dissatisfaction with the operational aspects of NATO's mission in Bosnia stemmed from his disdain for the United Nations' de facto veto power on use-of-force decisions—power derived from the dual-key agreement. On a number of occasions, NATO ground commanders called for strikes, only to be vetoed by UN civilian and political leaders. In some cases, the UN approval process took so long that once strikes were authorized, conditions on the ground had changed such that military strikes were no longer favored due to the different operational conditions. Wörner's dissatisfaction resulted in direct confrontations with Special Representative Yasushi Akashi, who held the United Nations' "key." Wörner would also speak with the United Nations' secretary general, Boutros Boutros-Ghali, in expressing his disappointment with the United Nations' military-enforcement role in Bosnia.[40] Wörner's public and private criticism of the United Nations earned him some political enemies among UN military leaders. It is noteworthy that the UN-PROFOR military commander, General Michael Rose, makes no mention of Wörner in his memoirs. Rose maintains that throughout 1994, NATO (in general) played a counterproductive role in the Balkans.[41]

On a personal level, Wörner and Joulwan always maintained re-

39. Ibid.
40. Hunter interview, July 7, 2003; Beard interview, August 4, 2003; senior NATO official "A" interview, September 23, 2003; Jonathan C. Randal, "Serbs Backing Off at NATO Deadline," Washington Post, April 24, 1994, A1.
41. General Sir Michael Rose, Fighting for Peace: Bosnia 1994 (London: Harville Press, 1998).

spect for each other, as they shared their frustration with the heavy role of the United Nations in Bosnia. At Wörner's urging, Joulwan would visit and brief him in the hospital in Aaken. When, at the conclusion of one visit in April 1994, Joulwan rose to leave the room, he turned to see Wörner struggling to rise from his sickbed. Despite Joulwan's request for him to remain in bed, Wörner noted his desire to "escort the SACEUR to the door."[42] Wörner's action suggests his high personal regard for Joulwan and is another illustration of the physical courage and passion for his role that he wished to demonstrate as NATO's secretary general.

In sum, the evidence indicates that as secretary general, Manfred Wörner was deeply involved in the military-operational aspects of NATO's policies in Bosnia, and he attempted to play an independent role in advocating for NATO military action. His efforts were impeded by the UN ground commanders and senior leaders, both of whom Wörner would lobby personally for different courses of action. In General Joulwan's view, Wörner's tendency for deep engagement in NATO's military affairs did not overstep his professional relationship with the SACEUR, mostly because the secretary general was ready to use force much earlier than all others at NATO, and was prepared to support the SACEUR in any policy movement toward increased military action. When the SACEUR made his case for more aggressive military stands against the Bosnian Serbs, Wörner backed him in the NAC, which is additional evidence of the close political partnership between NATO's civilian and political leaders over the issue of Bosnia.[43]

CONCLUSION

In nearly all of the previous scholarship on NATO's military actions in Bosnia, Secretary General Manfred Wörner barely surfaces in the historical record. This chapter demonstrates that Wörner played a critical role in developing NATO's policies on Bosnia, although at times his influence was severely constrained because of disagreements in the alliance.

42. Joulwan interview, October 27, 2003.
43. Ibid.

The systemic-political conditions in 1993 on Bosnia placed serious obstacles to policy change, which Wörner was unable to overcome in the short term. However, the idea that NATO would eventually have taken more aggressive steps in the absence of Manfred Wörner's leadership cannot be concluded with certainty. In 1993, among all the international political elite, Wörner was among the loudest advocates (and was perhaps the strongest advocate) for NATO military action in the Balkans. He lobbied aggressively for American leadership in NATO on the issue of Bosnia, and for military action against the Bosnian Serbs. In his view, NATO's appropriate post–Cold War role was to confront security crises like Bosnia. Although NATO never engaged in a sustained bombing campaign against the Bosnian Serbs while Wörner was alive, it did eventually adopt more hawkish policy solutions to the crisis, which culminated with Operation Deliberate Force in 1995. To discount the cumulative effects of Wörner's continued calls for NATO military action eliminates an important and respected voice in transnational security. Moreover, when the alliance moved to adopt more aggressive policy solutions during his time at NATO, the allies knew that Wörner would be supportive in his own distinctive and forceful way.

At the organizational level, principally within the NAC, Wörner's most important legacy on Bosnia is likely his presence at the April 1994 NAC meeting, when the NAC approved the expansion of the exclusion zones surrounding the UN safe havens in Goradze and elsewhere. Wörner also oversaw the NAC when it first threatened the use of force against the Serbs in February 1994 at the request of Boutros Boutros-Ghali, which is another important crossroads in NATO's post–Cold War evolution. Yet the April 1994 NAC decision stands out during Wörner's leadership tenure. His physical courage and his passion to protect NATO's credibility, while suffering from the intestinal cancer that took his life only four months later, left a lasting impression on all participants who witnessed him lead under such conditions. While no ambassador admits that Wörner "changed" votes in the NAC, the clear consensus among all senior officials interviewed is that Wörner's presence made a political difference in moving NATO toward action. More generally, Wörner was always viewed as an effective secretary general in the NAC, especially among the senior American political and military officials there at the time. Although his influence at the April 199..

NAC meeting is a more dramatic example of his leadership, it still squares with general impressions of his leadership and influence within the NAC during his tenure as secretary general.

Wörner's relations with the SACEUR and his general proclivity to grant NATO's military leaders discretion in determining how best to fulfill NATO's political mandate is also noteworthy. NATO military leaders never had to worry about going "too far" in implementing military actions that NATO had authorized. Such freedom granted the SACEUR and his subordinates the opportunity to act when they felt it was necessary, without concern that they would later face the political reprimand of the secretary general. At the same time, Wörner also expressed his operational concerns to the SACEUR frequently, as he called for more aggressive enforcement of NAC decisions and voiced his disappointment with the United Nations' military role in Bosnia. As in the two leadership forums discussed above, the evidence suggests again an aggressive secretary general, who attempted to shape alliance policy independently. Wörner's relations with the SACEUR demonstrate a high level of cooperation between the political and military leadership at NATO.

In sum, much evidence indicates that when examining NATO's conduct in the Balkans, Manfred Wörner's leadership of the organization cannot be dismissed, and in some cases was instrumental in moving the alliance toward military action. Wörner was not the only reason for NATO's more aggressive stands in 1994, but he does appear to have played a critical role in shaping NATO's agenda over the long term, within the NAC, and by giving his military subordinates political discretion and freedom to operate in Bosnia. Wörner's legacy had an important effect in shaping the systemic conditions for his successor, Willy Claes.

3

Willy Claes and Operation Deliberate Force

Willy Claes became NATO's secretary general in 1994, when the alliance was in crisis. Although NATO had begun the process of transforming itself through its Partnership for Peace program by reaching out to the former communist states of Central and Eastern Europe, the humanitarian tragedy in the Balkans threatened the political credibility of the alliance. Despite Manfred Wörner's valiant efforts to encourage American military leadership within the alliance, NATO continued to refrain from any sustained combat through the first half of 1995. When the alliance finally took aggressive action through Operation Deliberate Force, however, the two-week bombing campaign against the Bosnian Serbs brought the warring factions to the peace table in Dayton, Ohio. These events marked a significant change in NATO's role in transatlantic security and, arguably, saved the alliance from irrelevance.

In the historical analyses of NATO's post–Cold War evolution and the sustained military strikes in 1995, Secretary General Willy Claes is barely mentioned. Most journalistic attention to Claes has been devoted to his association with a bribery scandal stemming from his earlier days in Belgian politics, which eventually forced his departure from NATO. While the scandal had an important impact on his tenure as secretary general, other aspects of his leadership in the North Atlantic Council and with the SACEUR during Operation Deliberate Force provide important insights into Claes's critical role in the alliance. As demonstrated in this chapter, Claes played an instrumental role in Deliberate Force, and, more broadly, he must be recognized as a player in shaping NATO's post–Cold War transformation.

WILLY CLAES, 1994–1995

Belgian Willy Claes was appointed NATO's eighth secretary general on September 29, 1994—soon after the death of his highly revered predecessor, Manfred Wörner. Given the wide international and personal respect for Wörner, following in his footsteps would have been a difficult task for any new secretary general.

Before his term at NATO, Claes's political career began in his hometown, Haslet, Belgium, where he was elected a member of the City Council. In 1968, Claes was elected to Belgium's House of Representatives as a member of the country's Socialist Party. While in the majority party over the course of his political career, Claes served in an array of governmental ministerial positions, which included appointments as minister of education in 1972 and minister of economic affairs in 1973. He also served as deputy prime minister on five occasions and as minister of economic affairs two additional times. His international stature increased, however, when he served as minister of foreign affairs under the government of Prime Minister Jean-Luc Dehaene from 1992 until his selection as NATO's secretary general in 1994. While Claes was foreign minister, Belgium held the presidency of the European Union during the second half of 1993, which helped Claes's candidacy for secretary general considerably.

Upon Wörner's death, Claes surfaced quickly as a potential replacement. Others who were mentioned include Norwegian Thorvald Stoltenberg and Dutchman Hans van den Broek. Prime Minister Giuliano Amato of Italy and Prime Minister Ruud Lubbers of the Netherlands were also mentioned, but quickly dropped from consideration. Van den Broek's candidacy was also short lived, because of lackluster support from France. France actively backed Claes because of his previous support for a stronger "EU" common foreign and security policy, which squared with France's long-held support for a more integrated Europe. Foreign Secretary Douglas Hurd of Britain also briefly surfaced as a potential contender, with some support from the United States and Germany—but Hurd himself supposedly had personal reservations about the position, and the United Kingdom's influence for its own candidate was limited because its Lord Carrington had previously held the position, prior to Wörner.[1]

The final issue for resolving Claes's selection centered on Stoltenberg's candidacy. Norway felt that Germany had promised to support a Norwegian candidate, but when Claes's momentum increased and Stoltenberg's chances decreased rapidly without German backing, both Norway and Denmark cooperated in a last-ditch effort to promote another Scandinavian, Foreign Minister Uffe Ellemann-Jensen of Denmark. With the Scandinavian countries isolated, however, and all the major powers supportive of Claes by mid-September 1994, the Scandinavians relented and the final consensus was reached for Claes. Although Claes was not considered a high-profile choice, he had gained the Europeans' respect as EU president for his strong negotiating and diplomatic skills. Moreover, his candidacy was almost certainly helped by the United Kingdom's previous veto of another Belgian, Prime Minister Jean-Luc Dehaene, who was considered earlier in 1994 as a candidate for president of the European Union Commission. A second veto of a Belgian candidate would have been considered impolitic by many Europeans. Although Claes had already demonstrated that he had "an occasional short fuse," which would surface again when he served as secretary general, he clearly entered NATO with a solid reputation in foreign affairs.[2]

As noted earlier, much of Claes's legacy has been overshadowed

1. John Carvel, "Three-Horse Race Develops for Post of NATO Leader," *Guardian* (London), September 2, 1994, 10; Justin Burke, "At a Crossroads, NATO Moves Slowly on Choosing Leader," *Christian Science Monitor,* August 24, 1994, 3; George Brock, "France Draws Closer to NATO As Belgian Is Tipped for Next Leader," *Times* (London), September 12, 1994; "US to Back Belgian Foreign Minister for Top NATO Job," *Guardian* (London), September 16, 1994, 12.

2. Quotation from Lionel Barber, "EU Presidency Success Gave Boost to Claes," *Financial Times,* September 27, 1994, 2. See also "NATO's Gloomy Choice," *Economist* 333 (October 1, 1994): 65; "Willy Claes Most Likely New Head of NATO," *Agence France Presse,* September 13, 1994; Andrew Marshall, "Battle Looms over Top Job in NATO As Danes Step In," *Independent* (London), September 19, 1994, 14; and Chris Mclaughlin, "Battle Brewing over Top Job at Atlantic Alliance," *Scotsman,* September 24, 1994.

by his involvement in a bribery scandal over Belgian defense purchases that benefited his Socialist political party—a scandal that eventually forced his early exit from NATO headquarters. Much like Wörner, however, Claes played a critical role within the NAC on the issue of Bosnia, and he was especially instrumental in helping NATO succeed in its first sustained bombing campaign in 1995.

Systemic Conditions Facing Claes

Just as Manfred Wörner experienced, Claes inherited NATO's leadership position when the alliance, the Clinton administration, and members of the European Union were all struggling to define their post–Cold War foreign policies, especially as they related to the Bosnia crisis. Although NATO had conducted a number of small bombing operations to protect UNPROFOR troops and in response to Serb violations of no-fly zones prior to Claes's arrival, the major states of the world still held contrasting positions on the Balkan crisis and generally held firm on their preference for the United Nations having the lead role in Bosnia.[3] Although the alliance had taken steps under Wörner's leadership to increase the potential for military intervention, until the massacre of approximately seven thousand Bosnian Muslim men and boys by Bosnian Serb militias in July 1995, the United States refrained from exercising assertive leadership in NATO, mostly owing to the Clinton administration's unwillingness to support any sort of serious or sustained troop engagement in the Balkans.[4]

Like Wörner, Claes also was limited by the extensive political

3. Sonia Lucarelli, *Europe and the Breakup of Yugoslavia: A Political Failure in Search of a Scholarly Explanation* (The Hague: Kluwer Law International, 2000); James Gow, *Triumph of the Lack of Will: International Diplomacy and the Yugoslav War* (New York: Columbia University Press, 1997); David Rohde, *Endgame* (New York: Farrar, Straus and Giroux, 1997). Prior to Deliberate Force, besides the two NATO strikes discussed in Chapter 2, very limited NATO air strikes were conducted in 1994 on August 5, September 22, November 21, and November 23. In 1995, similar strikes occurred on May 25 and 26 and August 4.

4. David Halberstam, *War in a Time of Peace: Bush, Clinton and the Generals* (New York: Scribner, 2001), 303–18; Douglas C. Foyle, "Public Opinion and Bosnia: Anticipating Disaster," in *Contemporary Cases in U.S. Foreign Policy*, ed. Ralph G. Carter (Washington, DC: Congressional Quarterly, Inc., 2002), 32–58.

influence exercised by the United Nations on Bosnia. Claes and NATO ground commanders were constrained by the "dual-key" arrangement that had been negotiated between the United Nations and NATO in August 1993. Upon Claes's arrival to NATO, Special Representative Yasushi Akashi still held the United Nations' trigger and continued to exercise much restraint for using force.[5] Although the UN mission was the target of extensive criticism, until late July 1995, the center of diplomatic and policy action on Bosnia remained at the United Nations.

Willy Claes's personal political scandal, which overshadowed nearly all of his leadership period as secretary general, had relevance at the systemic level. Early in Claes's tenure as secretary general, in February 1995, he was accused of having knowledge of bribes received on behalf of his former Belgian Socialist Party from the Italian defense firm Agusta in 1988, during his earlier days in Belgian ministerial politics. When these accusations became public, Claes initially indicated that he had no knowledge of the bribes, with specific statements made to all NATO ambassadors in private that he knew nothing of these events. Soon after his first comments, however, he was forced to admit that he did know of the events, although he maintained that he had not approved of the bribes. His association with bribes damaged his international reputation and ended his tenure as secretary general after only thirteen months.[6] Although Claes's problems were "personal" in nature, the bribery issue became international news and thus became part of the systemic conditions in which he operated.

Claes's damaged international stature paralleled critics' assessment of NATO more generally, as the alliance was proving unable to mitigate the deepening humanitarian crisis in Bosnia. In 1994 NATO initiated the Partnership for Peace program, which created partnerships between the newly formed democracies of Central and Eastern Europe and the NATO allies in an attempt to assist

5. Lt. Col. Ronald M. Reed, "Chariots of Fire: Rules of Engagement in Operation Deliberate Force," in *Deliberate Force: A Case Study in Effective Air Campaigning,* ed. Col. Robert C. Owen (Maxwell Air Force Base, AL: Air University Press, 2000), 402–3.

6. Craig R. Whitney, "Facing Charges, NATO Head Steps Down," *New York Times,* October 21, 1995, A5; Paul Belien, "Meanwhile, in Europe's Arkansas," *National Review* 47, 3 (March 20, 1995): 30.

the new democracies in their democratization and military-professionalization efforts. At the beginning of 1995, the alliance also initiated a study of membership enlargement, which was the first formal step taken to indicate an interest in expanding the alliance. Although NATO was showing clear signs of evolution to meet the new, post–Cold War security environment, these changes were being overshadowed by its powerlessness on Bosnia. The alliance generally remained hesitant to become engaged. Claes's damaged reputation, in some respects, seemed symbolic of an alliance that was plagued by credibility problems. His personal political problems also likely created disincentives for Claes to go public in his appeals for policy change, given the already intensive media scrutiny directed toward his personal problems.

In sum, Claes faced a host of international systemic constraints on his leadership maneuverability. Ongoing political disagreements between the United States and the European countries, including the absence of American leadership on Bosnia, made it difficult for Claes to steer NATO in a new policy direction had he wanted to. Moreover, his own personal political problems, when coupled with the high stature of predecessor Manfred Wörner, added another systemic limitation on what Claes could do to implement change. The omnipresent role of the United Nations and the existing dual-key framework likewise provided additional systemic barriers on what Claes could attempt. Certainly, the international criticism directed at NATO and the severity of the humanitarian problems in the Balkans created both political and even moral reasons for action, but not until late July 1995 did the transatlantic momentum shift toward more aggressive military options, which later empowered Claes in the NAC.

Under the systemic circumstances of the second half of 1994 and the first six months of 1995, most of the evidence indicates that Claes decided to cautiously lead the alliance. He did not attempt to aggressively challenge the political limitations he faced, and his caution was most clearly witnessed in the first months of his leadership. Individuals who worked at NATO note that Claes was reserved initially, both personally and publicly, upon becoming secretary general, and was hesitant to show his policy preferences. Leif Mevik, former NATO ambassador from Norway, notes that Claes seemed "nervous" in his initial meeting with the ambassadors, and that his style remained "uncertain" when he first became the secretary general. In his inaugural address at NATO headquarters, Claes barely mentioned the rapidly deteriorating conditions in the Balkans. In his first substantive speech as secretary general, he buried near the end of his address a comment on Bosnia and the United Nations as he noted, "Basically, our cooperation with the United Nations has gone smoothly"—a statement that ran counter to nearly all journalistic evidence at the time.[7] Claes's initially reserved leadership style was likely a reflection of the systemic realities, in that no transatlantic policy consensus existed, despite the escalating humanitarian crisis in Bosnia. Claes's decision to refrain from steering the alliance in a different policy direction stands in stark contrast to the efforts of Wörner, who from the start of the crisis was pressuring the allies to intervene.

As the situation in the Balkans worsened in 1995, however, some evidence indicates that Claes recognized that use-of-force options would be needed in order to address the situation, and his assertiveness increased. Claes began to more publicly support such policy proposals, which by that time corresponded with the policy preferences of the Clinton administration, especially as the United States moved toward military options in the summer of 1995. To some extent, Claes was ahead of the Clinton administration, in that he much earlier recognized the need for military options.[8] In January 1995, Claes noted that Bosnia "has been a source for scourge for Europe and for the organizations which have become involved with it." In early 1995, he also began to reiterate publicly that "NATO

7. Leif Mevik, *Det nye NATO: en personlig beretning* [New NATO: A Personal Narrative] (Bergen: Eide, 1999), English translation provided in correspondence with author by Mevik, January 31, 2003; Daniel Christman, former U.S. military representative to NATO, phone interview with author, July 16, 2002; senior U.S. Department of Defense official "A," phone interview with author, June 28, 2002; Willy Claes, "Speech by the Secretary General to the Press on Arrival at NATO HQ," October 17, 1994, NATO, http://www.nato.int/docu/speech/1994/s941017a.htm, and "The 40th General Assembly of the Atlantic Treaty Association, The Hague, The Netherlands," October 28, 1994, NATO, http://www.nato.int/docu/speech/1994/s941028.htm.

8. Robert Hunter, former U.S. ambassador to NATO, phone interview with author, July 16, 2002; George Joulwan, former SACEUR, phone interview with author, January 2003; senior NATO official "A," phone interview with author, October 15, 2002.

is more than a sub-contractor of the UN," and that he shared "the frustrations and the impatience of the critics when it comes to ap-plying pressures to resolve the Bosnian war."[9] In this regard, Claes was preparing the alliance for a much broader use of force than the allies were contemplating through much of 1995.

At the same time, Claes's actions were never openly out of synch with the American position. Unlike Wörner, Claes was careful not to challenge the United States specifically to lead the alliance. Former American national security advisor Anthony Lake maintains that Claes was never viewed as an obstacle by the United States in mov-ing the alliance toward military action in 1995, and that he was a helpful advocate for the American position. Another key partici-pant noted that from the American perspective, Claes was always on "the right side of the issue, as far as we were concerned."[10] In contrast to Wörner, who actively encouraged NATO intervention into the Balkans in numerous public appearances, Claes was more reserved in openly calling for NATO strikes, which some at NATO considered a wise diplomatic move given the existing systemic con-straints.[11]

In dealing more specifically with the United Nations' role in the Balkans, Claes was helpful in moving NATO's agenda toward more aggressive military options in 1995. Claes criticized the United Na-tions and the dual-key framework, and would refer derogatorily to "the UN." As noted by one senior NATO official, Claes was a "viru-lent critic of the United Nations, both publicly and privately."[12] This position squared with the United States' position as dissatisfaction grew with the United Nations and UNPROFOR.

9. Willy Claes, "Speech by Mr. Willy Claes, Secretary General of NATO, to the 'Grandes Conferences Catholiques,'" January 9, 1995, NATO, http://www. nato.int/docu/speech/1995/s950109b.htm, and "Speech by the Sec-retary General at the Munich Security Conference," February 3, 1995, NATO, http:// www.nato.int/docu/speech/1995/s950203a.htm.

10. Anthony Lake, former U.S. national security advisor, phone interview with author, July 15, 2002; senior U.S. Department of Defense official "A" in-terview, June 28, 2002.

11. Lambert Willem Veenendaal, former Netherlands ambassador to NATO, phone interview with author, July 23, 2003.

12. Senior U.S. Department of Defense official "A" interview, June 28, 2002; senior NATO official "A" interview, October 15, 2002.

When American pressure began to build for policy change in late
July 1995, one principal change was the transfer of the United Nations' key from Akashi to a UN field commander, General Bernard
Janvier of France. Though he was an advocate for and supporter of
this policy change, Claes cannot be credited with achieving this result alone. Yet his was certainly another voice, along with the United
States', that was helpful in removing the key from Akashi, who was
viewed as too tentative in supporting military action and too closely
tied to the United Nations' secretary general, Boutros Boutros-
Ghali. In this respect, Claes helped empower NATO vis-à-vis the
United Nations and eventually helped shift the center of diplomatic
and military attention to NATO.

Claes's association with the bribery charge clearly damaged his
international reputation and his potential for individual policy entrepreneurship—although reaction to this scandal inside NATO headquarters was mixed. While Claes was still in office, key participants
at nearly all senior policy-making levels in the United States, including the Joint Chiefs of Staff and the National Security Council,
and those among the allies' governments as well, were concerned
that Claes's personal political problems would damage his ability to
lead.[13] Yet even though senior policy makers were concerned about
Claes's weakened condition, the accusations did not destroy him
politically in the short term. Some evidence suggests that Claes's
power actually increased in NATO, especially in relation to the
Americans, since many saw the accusations as part and parcel of
Belgian politics—viewed by many as corrupt, petty, and parochial.
Since Claes was no longer directly involved in Belgian domestic
politics, it was felt by some that he was the Belgian Socialists' political scapegoat.[14] For example, in his memoirs about the Dayton Peace
Accords, Richard Holbrooke, who was then the U.S. assistant secretary of state for European and Canadian affairs, expressed doubt
about the validity of the bribery charges. Leif Mevik writes similarly, "We who were close to him the year he was NATO's Secretary
General, avoided forming definite opinions about his possible guilt

13. Christman interview, July 16, 2002; Lake interview, July 15, 2002; Mevik
correspondence with author, January 31, 2003.
14. Senior U.S. Department of Defense official "A" interview, June 28, 2002;
Thomas Montgomery, former U.S. military representative to NATO, phone interview with author, August 15, 2002.

or innocence. That question was up to the Courts to decide. This said, I believe we felt at the bottom of our hearts that Claes was not 'criminal' who willingly and consciously had 'enriched himself' in the Agusta affair."[15] Thus, Claes's domestic political problems translated into sympathy from some allies, especially the Americans, who felt that Claes was treated unfairly but that he weathered the political storm admirably.

These "kinder" views of Claes should not be read to imply that he went unscathed by the accusations. Some ambassadors note that the scandal proved damaging to Claes's ability to lead the alliance, simultaneously tarnishing NATO's credibility at a time when it badly needed legitimacy.[16] Although the European allies considered the accusations more serious than did the Americans, it appears that few doubted Claes's commitment to seeing the alliance succeed in Bosnia. The consensus view is that Claes was still able to lead the alliance internally prior to and during Operation Deliberate Force, although the allies recognized that his association with bribery would eventually force his removal from office.[17] At minimum, however, the concerns expressed by many at NATO over Claes's political problems suggest the inherent importance of the secretary general. If Claes had been an irrelevant actor in the alliance, his political problems would not have generated concern from the member states.

In sum, Claes operated under challenging systemic conditions, which made it difficult for him to have an independent impact on the alliance. Most evidence suggests that he chose not to resist these systemic constraints, and that he instead decided to cautiously lead the alliance. Unlike Wörner, Claes chose not to stand alone in calling for NATO intervention. Under such difficult systemic political conditions, Claes could have done little to affect transatlantic political views on Bosnia. Rather, he waited to exercise greater influence within the North Atlantic Council, where his political power could be better utilized. His organizational influence in the NAC was far more substantial and meaningful on NATO's policies toward Bosnia.

15. Richard Holbrooke, *To End a War* (New York: Random House, 1998), 120; Mevik correspondence with author, January 31, 2003.

16. John Anderson, former Canadian ambassador to NATO, phone interview with author, July 16, 2003; Veenendaal interview, July 23, 2003.

17. Senior NATO official "A" interview, October 2002.

Organizational Leadership

As noted earlier, the allies continued to struggle over how to address Bosnia for the first half of 1995. Major steps in changing policy toward Bosnia occurred at the July 1995 London Summit, where the major allies in NATO and the United Nations adopted more aggressive use-of-force policy options. Many of the operational details from the summit, however, needed additional refinement and explication. The necessary policy articulation fell upon NATO's North Atlantic Council.

At a series of NAC meetings in late July and early August, NATO agreed to use force to protect the Bosnian city of Goradze if it came under attack from the Bosnian Serbs. Also, NATO and the United Nations decided to remove the UN key for using force from Yasushi Akashi and give it to an UNPROFOR ground commander, General Bernard Janvier. The NAC also established three sets of targets, known as "Options," allowing NATO to strike Option I and II targets upon the next provocation from the Bosnian Serbs. These targets included Serbian air-defense systems located in southeastern Bosnia and other Bosnian Serb military sites. In a meeting on August 1, the NAC added other UN "safe enclaves" besides Goradze to NATO's protective jurisdiction.[18]

Comments from interviews conducted with key participants indicate that Claes played an important role in moving the alliance toward use-of-force options at these council sessions, especially at one "marathon session" held on July 25, 1995. Claes did a number of things that helped shape the agenda, while fostering consensus within the alliance. He was infamous for keeping NAC meetings in session regardless of the time. Claes exercised a great deal of discretionary power over time and the meeting atmosphere. The council's crucial meeting on July 25 to work for policy consensus within the alliance went on for thirteen hours. Claes's determination, his control of time, and his commitment to find consensus assisted the alliance in adopting more aggressive military options. During such long sessions, Claes was known for bringing all the issues into the

18. Reed, "Chariots of Fire," 406–7. See also Ivo H. Daalder, *Getting to Dayton: The Making of America's Bosnia Policy* (Washington, DC: Brookings Institution Press, 2000), 77–79.

open, so that there was little confusion on what states were agreeing to, and for demanding that states take policy positions. Under Claes's leadership, the NAC meetings were also very orderly, as he would continue to keep the ambassadors focused on the issue at hand. Claes's style was unambiguous, with great attention to detail.[19]

As the alliance debated policy changes at these NAC meetings, former U.S. ambassador to NATO Robert Hunter maintains, Claes's diplomatic style and his support for the United States' position were helpful in terms of agenda setting and moving some of NATO's European allies, especially the Netherlands and Norway, toward military options. Claes also worked closely with the Greek and Turkish delegations at NATO in efforts to build and maintain their support for the bombing campaign to come. NATO works by consensus, so gaining the support of all member states, regardless of a state's military contribution to the alliance, is essential for making policy. Claes's open and vocal support of military options, which at times in August 1995 was even more aggressive than that of the senior Clinton administration officials, was likely important in winning some of the European allies over to the Americans' preferred policies.[20]

Another aspect of Claes's influence in the NAC was the diplomatic style he used in meetings, which occasionally consisted of theatrics. Despite initial impressions of his leadership style as reserved and tentative, he later became known at NATO headquarters for his temperamental outbursts, which would be invoked when necessary to promote consensus. Wörner's "booming" voice is remembered by many, and Claes's near tantrums are similarly recalled. Such outbursts were not common, but would occur when an ally began to balk about past commitments. Mevik notes that Claes was "short tempered," and that he once witnessed Claes "explode in rage" at a NATO defense ministers meeting.[21] Key participants felt that Claes's diplomatic theatrics and strong temper were effective in

19. Senior U.S. Department of Defense official "A" interview, June 28, 2002; Montgomery interview, August 15, 2002.

20. Hunter interview, July 16, 2002; former SACEUR George Joulwan, phone interviews with author, October 2002 and January 2003; senior U.S. Department of Defense official "A" interview, June 28, 2002.

21. Mevik correspondence with author, January 31, 2003.

promoting consensus, in that ambassadors did not want to become the recipient of his venting.[22]

Besides these examples of Claes's leadership of the NAC, three specific cases of his organizational leadership stand out. It is first noteworthy that prior to Claes's entry as secretary general, many of the legal parameters involving military decisions for NATO were already set. The UN Security Council—most importantly through Resolution 836, passed on June 4, 1993—had authorized NATO to use force to protect UN peacekeepers. The Security Council had also authorized NATO to use force for violations of the no-fly zones over certain areas of Bosnia.[23] Once Claes was in office, the important evolutionary changes in policy came at the NAC meetings after the London Summit in July 1995, when it was agreed that a UN ground commander, General Janvier, would hold the United Nations' "key." The commander in chief of Allied Forces Southern Europe, who was now Admiral Leighton Smith, still held NATO's "key." The change in key at the United Nations signaled a new willingness to use force if any party violated the United Nations' international agreements. In this sense, Claes was not intended to be a central decision maker on initiating force: these decisions were delegated to Janvier and Smith.

On August 28, 1995, when a mortar was fired on Sarajevo that killed thirty-eight civilians, the dual-key decision process went into motion. After a brief investigation, NATO and the United Nations determined that the Bosnian Serbs were responsible. General Janvier, who was away at his son's wedding, had temporarily relinquished his key to Lieutenant General Rupert Smith of Britain. Rupert Smith and Admiral Leighton Smith both turned their keys without debate. Janvier returned immediately and supported Rupert Smith's decision.[24] These decisions put into motion the strikes that

22. Montgomery interview, August 15, 2002; senior U.S. Department of Defense official "A," phone interview with author, August 13, 2002.

23. For the full range of Security Council decisions, see Jane Boulden, *Peace Enforcement: The United Nations Experience in Congo, Somalia, and Bosnia* (Westport, CT: Praeger, 2001), 83–95.

24. Rick Atkinson, "Air Assault Set Stage for Broader Role," *Washington Post*, November 15, 1995, A1; David L. Dittmer and Stephen P. Dawkins, *Deliberate Force: NATO's First Extended Air Operation* (Alexandria, VA: Center for Naval Analyses, 1998), 20–21; Tim Ripley, *Operation Deliberate Force* (Lancaster, UK: CDISS, 1999), 242–44.

came only hours later, in the early morning hours of August 30, and became known as Operation Deliberate Force.

Prima facie, little input could be expected from Claes, given that the dual-key decision-making procedures had already been defined. Moreover, then SACEUR General George Joulwan maintains that he and Claes both understood that once both keys were turned, a military response would follow.[25] In his memoirs of these events, however, Richard Holbrooke gives Willy Claes considerable credit for *not* initiating a NAC meeting prior to the use of force in the few hours before Deliberate Force. Holbrooke notes that Claes's decision not to convene the council was crucial, in that it avoided launching additional policy debate within NATO and allowed the bombing campaign to ensue. With sixteen members in NATO at the time, additional policy differences certainly could have been raised if a meeting had been called. While it appears that most of the alliance was already committed to using force, Claes prevented discussion at the political level in Brussels by allowing the bombings to proceed absent a NAC meeting.[26] While Claes's role was ancillary to the decisions made on the ground by the "dual-key" decision makers, he clearly exercised his discretionary authority not to call a meeting, and thus played an important role in moving the alliance toward the military strikes.

Another important example of Claes's leadership occurred on September 1, when General Bernard Janvier, with support from Admiral Leighton Smith and Richard Holbrooke, requested a cease-fire in order to negotiate with the Bosnian Serbs. Claes was not involved in these decisions. Where Claes became important, however, was in the effort to restart the bombings as soon as possible. When the cease-fire lasted longer than Claes, Holbrooke, Joulwan, and others wanted, Claes personally phoned Janvier, who was responsible for granting the extended cease-fire. In what has been characterized as Claes's "rage" over Janvier's decision, the secretary general expressed profound disagreement with the cease-fire that Ratko Mladic, Bosnian Serb military commander, had negotiated with Janvier. Former U.S. ambassador to NATO Robert Hunter maintains that Claes was instrumental at this time in placing additional responsibility on

25. Joulwan interview, January 2003.
26. Holbrooke, *To End a War,* 99; senior U.S. Department of Defense official "A" interview, August 13, 2002.

UNPROFOR leaders for the cease-fire, noting that they would be blamed by the international community for a failure in Bosnia.[27] Although this example applies equally to his efforts to influence the systemic political conditions, his dialogue with Janvier certainly set the stage for his organizational leadership that came the following day.

A third example of Claes's leadership occurred on September 2, when the NAC reconvened to discuss the negotiated cease-fire. Claes announced that the ambassadors were not there to debate whether or not to use force, but rather to decide what length of a cease-fire to permit. Claes is credited with making an important decision at the organizational level, in that he defined the appropriate military option for the alliance.[28] Ambiguity within the NAC at this time was possible, given the rapidly changing events and the unknown political territory that NATO had entered as an alliance.[29] In this regard, Claes exercised considerable authority through this interpretation of his power as secretary general, and this was a factor in resuming the bombings on September 4. The bombings continued until September 14, when the initial peace negotiations began prior to what eventually became the Dayton Peace Accords.

In sum, Claes's leadership of the NAC stands in contrast to his much less influential role at the systemic level. Both in the initiation of Operation Deliberate Force and in resuming the air strikes, the evidence suggests that Claes was very important in promoting alliance consensus and in moving NATO toward military action. For his own leadership style in council meetings and the exercise of his discretionary powers as secretary general, Claes deserves some credit for moving the alliance toward use-of-force options at a time when NATO's credibility was at stake and the humanitarian conditions in Bosnia were worsening daily. While a consensus had already been achieved among the allies that NATO military action was necessary in the Balkans, it helped that Claes actively promoted this consen-

27. Quotation from Rick Atkinson, "In Almost Losing Its Resolve, NATO Alliance Found Itself," *Washington Post,* November 16, 1995, A1; Joulwan interview, January 2003; Hunter interview, July 16, 2002.

28. Holbrooke, *To End a War,* 120; Col. Robert C. Owen, "Summary," in *Deliberate Force: A Case Study in Effective Air Campaigning,* 499.

29. Hunter interview, July 16, 2002; senior U.S. Department of Defense official "A" interview, August 13, 2002.

sus. Much like Wörner, Claes was able to capitalize on his chairmanship of the NAC to exercise greater leadership of the allies than might ordinarily have been in his purview. Similarly, an examination of Claes's relationship with NATO's supreme allied commander suggests important examples of leadership during his tenure.

Working with the SACEUR: Claes and George Joulwan

During Claes's entire period of service as secretary general, General George Joulwan served as NATO's supreme allied commander, Europe (SACEUR). An examination of Claes's working relationship with Joulwan is useful, both for understanding Claes's role in military affairs and for historical insights, especially given that Operation Deliberate Force was the first sustained military campaign the alliance had ever conducted. An examination of the development of NATO's strategic-bombing plan and target-selection process provides some insight into this element of Claes's leadership.

It is worth recalling first that no research has linked Claes to any element of NATO's military campaign on the Bosnian Serbs. To some extent, this might be expected, given that the SACEUR is charged with NATO's military planning, and given the extensive role played by the United Nations in Bosnia in 1995. In fact, much of the historical evidence generally supports the idea that Claes's voice was limited in terms of developing NATO's military plans. The military strategy and bombing plans were created in the months preceding Operation Deliberate Force by a joint NATO-UN planning board.[30] After the Bosnian Serb attacks on Sarajevo in August 1995, when Deliberate Force became a reality and the keys were turned by both the United Nations' Bernard Janvier and NATO's Leighton Smith, it was Janvier and Smith who debated over the first set of targets to hit. When the bombing campaign proceeded, Admiral Smith delegated all tactical decisions to General Michael Ryan of the United States, commander of Allied Air Forces Southern Europe, while Joulwan provided the strategic direction and guidance for the mission. The aircraft used, targets, sequence, and timing were determined

30. Christopher M. Campbell, "The Deliberate Force Air Campaign Plan," in *Deliberate Force: A Case Study in Effective Air Campaigning,* 99–110.

by General Ryan, who closely protected his authority and shielded himself from extensive political access.[31] This evidence suggests that Claes was removed from much of NATO's military planning, as General Ryan made many of the tactical decisions for the alliance.

At the same time, however, SACEUR Joulwan notes that Claes had detailed knowledge of the bombing strategy and was privy to the operational plans of Deliberate Force well before the operation ensued. On two occasions, Claes and Joulwan met before the operation began and discussed at length the proposed military strategy, should one become necessary. One meeting between Claes and Joulwan took place at the NATO air base in Villa Franca, Italy, and another in Claes's office at NATO headquarters shortly before the bombings. In these planning phases, Claes allowed Joulwan considerable leeway in determining the appropriate military action—within the constraints of the various options that the NAC had authorized. Joulwan views Claes's decision to grant him some independence in exercising military judgments as very helpful in achieving NATO's eventual success.[32] Additional evidence suggests that even during NAC sessions prior to the strikes, Claes worked closely with the SACEUR, who pushed the alliance for "clarity," that is, detailed and specific instructions should military action become reality.[33]

Claes's cooperation with the SACEUR at NAC meetings once the bombings began is another important yet overlooked aspect of civil-military leadership relations during the campaign. Because of Joulwan's sometimes forceful personality, the new type of mission that NATO was about to initiate, and the Europeans' distaste for strong American leadership at NATO, the European allies viewed

31. Mark A. Bucknam, "The Influence of UN and NATO Theater–Level Commanders on the Use of Airpower over Bosnia during Deny Flight: 1993–1995" (Ph.D. diss., King's College, 1999), 209–12; John C. Orndorff, "Aspects of Leading and Following: The Human Factors of Deliberate Force," in *Deliberate Force: A Case Study in Effective Air Campaigning*, 355–57. See also Mark J. Conversino, "Executing Deliberate Force, 30 August–14 September 1995," in *Deliberate Force: A Case Study in Effective Air Campaigning*, 132–33.

32. Joulwan interview, October 2002.

33. Senior NATO official "A," phone interview with author, October 15, 2002.

Joulwan with some suspicion.[34] To quell these concerns, Joulwan consulted extensively with the NAC during the bombing campaign on all aspects of the operation. When Joulwan attended NAC meetings, Claes would occasionally ask him tough and detailed operational questions. Claes raised such questions, however, not necessarily because of his own concerns, but rather to serve as a proxy voice for allies who did not want to raise their doubts in a council session with the SACEUR.[35] In doing this, Claes gave "political cover" to any ambassador who wished to question the operations without openly showing opposition to the SACEUR or to any of the other allies who favored vigorous military action. In this regard, Claes worked to reduce political and military ambiguity between the council and the SACEUR, and fostered consensus by serving as a proxy voice for those allies who had real concerns.

Claes's most significant operational-military role in Deliberate Force, however, came through his decision not to consult the NAC before NATO's use of Tomahawk missiles in northern Bosnia, near Banja Luka, on September 10. While these strikes officially fit within the previously agreed upon Option II targeting plans, some NATO ambassadors expressed considerable opposition afterwards on the use of Tomahawks, which was viewed by some as escalatory and a violation of the SACEUR's authority. The state expressing the greatest concern was France, followed by Canada, Greece, and Spain. The strikes also took place outside of the "southeast zone of action," which some NATO members viewed as the principal authorized area of military targeting.[36]

The request to use the Tomahawks came from General Ryan. Among NATO military officials, it was clearly understood that the use of Tomahawks was a possible overextension of the mandate

---

34. Senior U.S. Department of Defense official "A" interview, June 28, 2002; General Sir Michael Rose, *Fighting for Peace: Bosnia 1994* (London: Harville Press, 1998), 122–23. See also George Graham and Jurek Martin, "Joulwan Named to Head NATO Forces," *Financial Times*, October 5, 1993, 7.

35. Hunter interview, July 16, 2002; senior U.S. Department of Defense official "A" interview, June 28, 2002; senior NATO official "A" interview, October 15, 2002.

36. Holbrooke, *To End a War*, 143; Rick Atkinson and Daniel Williams, "NATO Rejects Demand to End Bombing; Russia Warns Alliance on Bosnia Campaign," *Washington Post*, September 12, 1995, A1.

given to the SACEUR.[37] In recognizing the potential political problems that the Tomahawks could cause, General Joulwan did not immediately approve General Ryan's request, but rather waited thirty-six hours in order to gain political approval from the secretary general.[38]

Claes's relevance and importance here is, first, that he knew of the Tomahawk strikes in advance. In this respect, Claes was an integral part of the decision to use the missiles, which has been viewed by some military analysts as a strategically critical military maneuver in demonstrating NATO's advanced military capabilities to the Bosnian Serbs. Richard Holbrooke notes that "the psychological effect of such sophisticated weapons, previously used only in the Gulf War, was enormous." The extent to which the Tomahawks had an impact on the war will always be an issue in question, yet there is clear evidence that a number of top American foreign-policy officials felt that the Tomahawks were quite significant in ending the war.[39]

Second, Claes demonstrated his power by supporting the SACEUR's and General Ryan's military judgment without consulting the council. Joulwan's discussions with Claes on the Tomahawks occurred on a weekend, when many NATO ambassadors were not readily available in Brussels.[40] At the same time, in NATO's first sustained bombing campaign ever, Joulwan's communication with Claes and the thirty-six-hour notice given to the secretary general would certainly have allowed Claes ample opportunity to call an emergency meeting or, at minimum, to phone key allied ambas-

37. Tim Ripley, *Operation Deliberate Force: The UN and NATO Campaign in Bosnia, 1995* (Lancaster, UK: CDISS, 1999), 281.

38. Joulwan interview, January 2003.

39. Holbrooke, *To End a War,* 143. This view is also held by Admiral Leighton Smith, former commander in chief of NATO Allied Forces Southern Europe. See Owen, "Summary," in *Deliberate Force: A Case Study in Effective Air Campaigning,* 491–92; and Conversino, "Executing Deliberate Force, 30 August–14 September 1995," in *Deliberate Force: A Case Study in Effective Air Campaigning,* 153. On this broader debate, see Robert A. Pape, "The True Worth of Air Power," *Foreign Affairs* 83, no. 2 (2004): 122–23; and Michael Horowitz and Dan Reiter, "When Does Aerial Bombing Work?" *Journal of Conflict Resolution* 45, no. 2 (2001): 167.

40. Joulwan interview, January 2003. See also Bucknam, "The Influence of UN and NATO Theater-Level Commanders," 228.

sadors to notify them of the forthcoming missile strikes. Moreover, if the use of Tomahawks was viewed in American military circles as potentially controversial, it seems probable that Claes too understood their potential political significance. Claes did provide written notification to the ambassadors before the forthcoming Tomahawk strikes, but these written messages were not received until after the first strike.[41]

Claes called a NAC meeting early on the Monday after the strikes. Some ambassadors noted that they first heard about the attacks through a phone call early Monday morning from Claes or by seeing reports of the events televised on the Cable News Network (CNN). A number of ambassadors expressed serious concern about the use of Tomahawk missiles and also demanded improved communication methods for NATO.[42] Claes likely anticipated these reactions of opposition, and thus in choosing to allow the Tomahawks' use, he played an important role in supporting Joulwan's request for more vigorous military action from NATO. Had the council been notified in advance, a good chance exists that serious objections would have been raised and the use of those missiles may have been prohibited.

Thus, despite almost no mention of Claes's military leadership role during Deliberate Force in previous research, the evidence indicates that he had some influence in NATO's target selection. His decision to grant the SACEUR considerable leeway in military-tactical decisions, his knowledge of the entire military strategy, and his decision not to consult with the NAC prior to use of the Tomahawk missiles must be acknowledged when examining Claes's leadership of the alliance.

More broadly, on the civil-military relationship between NATO's political and military leaders, the evidence suggests that Claes deferred to Joulwan's military judgment but at the same time had full knowledge of the military plans for Deliberate Force. Claes's more "hands-off" approach vis-à-vis Joulwan is a bit different from the style of Wörner, who was more vocal in expressing his views on military matters. This difference may stem, in part, from Germany's

---

41. On the written notification, Joulwan interview, January 2003.

42. Ripley, *Operation Deliberate Force,* 286; senior NATO official "A" interview, October 15, 2002.

different political and military traditions, which encouraged and supported more active political oversight of the military in the aftermath of the Second World War. Wörner's more aggressive approach may also have been influenced by his extensive experience in defense issues, as compared to that of Claes, whose ministerial focus in the Belgian government was economic and diplomatic affairs. Whatever the cause for these differences, the evidence demonstrates that Claes's relations with General Joulwan represent a critical facet of Operation Deliberate Force.

CONCLUSION

NATO's first sustained bombing campaign, Operation Deliberate Force, involved a host of decision-makers, including both military and political leaders from the United Nations and NATO, as well as from the sixteen allied governments. Since NATO had never engaged in a military operation of this nature, it would have been difficult to predict what sort of role the NATO secretary general would play in this operation. Considering Cold War experience and the historical role(s) of the secretary general, along with the many leadership impediments that Willy Claes faced upon becoming NATO's political leader, it seems reasonable to expect that he would have been a minor, if not tertiary, player in the alliance's part of the operation. This chapter indicates otherwise, although Claes's influence varied, according to the leadership framework examined in this study.

The evidence demonstrates that at the systemic level, a multitude of international political obstacles prevented Claes from having an independent impact on the alliance. When Claes began to openly advocate his own views for military action against the Bosnian Serbs, his position corresponded with the general direction of American foreign policy. Moreover, as the Bosnia tragedy worsened, the political environment in which NATO operated also lent itself to leadership from the secretary general. NATO was in a political crisis and needed an effective demonstration of force in order to maintain its credibility in transatlantic security. The organization had entered an era filled with uncertainty and without precedent, and such an ambiguous political environment likely worked to Claes's advantage. If NATO was going to play a new role in post–Cold War security, the conditions in the Balkans would eventually demand action.

Inaction would have caused NATO's international stature to sink deeper and would have called into question the need for NATO. Yet up until the London Summit in July 1995, Claes remained on the political fringe and made little effort to publicly build momentum for a new policy direction.

Given that much of Claes's legacy at NATO is remembered in a negative light because of his association with the Agusta bribery scandal, it should also be recognized that Claes had personal political incentives to cooperate with the United States when the scandal became public. This crisis had a systemic impact, and limited what he could do to influence the international political debate on Bosnia. During the remainder of Claes's tenure in office, it was the United States that proved to be his best supporter, even though many at NATO viewed the accusations lodged against him as unfair. Had Claes been openly opposed to aggressive military options, it seems likely that the United States would have called for his removal. No evidence, however, suggests that Claes's personal view of the situation in the Balkans changed or adapted to the American view. In SACEUR Joulwan's words, Claes viewed Slobodan Milosevic as an "old school communist" who would only respond to military strikes.[43] Thus, Claes's support of NATO military action should not be equated with subservience to the United States' position. His public assertiveness corresponded with the changes in the systemic environment, as the United States and eventually the allies recognized the imminent need for military action in the Balkans.

Within the North Atlantic Council, Claes's leadership role was much more visible and influential. As council chairman, Claes seized on his own discretionary powers and skillfully employed diplomatic techniques in managing the allies to enhance his powers as secretary general. His refusal to call for a NAC meeting before Operation Deliberate Force and his determination that the council debate only *when* to resume the bombing while the cease-fire was in progress were important in keeping consensus among the allies. Again, without the United States' backing and readiness to use force, Claes would not have been able to exercise the influence he did in the council. Claes's personal diplomatic style, his occasional "outbursts" at NAC sessions, and his management of council meetings are all important elements of his organizational leadership. These

43. Joulwan interview, October 2002.

traits are clearly specific to Claes and contributed to his leadership role as secretary general. Much like Manfred Wörner's, Claes's ability to influence the wider political agenda came through leadership within the NAC.

In terms of his leadership and relationship with the SACEUR, the evidence demonstrates that Claes and Joulwan worked together closely to move the alliance toward military action. Claes's detailed knowledge of the bombing plans and, most importantly, his decision to allow the use of the Tomahawk missiles without consulting the NAC represent critical aspects of his leadership legacy and provide insight into his views on appropriate civil-military relations at NATO. Claes did not stand in the way of Joulwan's military judgment, which likely resulted from Joulwan's extensive consultations with Claes and the North Atlantic Council, as well as from Claes's own belief that tough military action was needed to defeat the Bosnian Serbs.

In sum, Willy Claes was an instrumental player at NATO as it adapted to new missions and roles in transatlantic security. Operation Deliberate Force was a revolutionary policy choice that helped NATO adapt to new security challenges after the Cold War. In some respects, this operation made possible the strikes on Milosevic in 1999 and Secretary General Javier Solana's role in leading NATO toward military action, which is the focus of Chapter 4.

4

Javier Solana and Operation Allied Force

On December 2, 1995, NATO chose Javier Solana, Spain's foreign minister, to replace Willy Claes as the alliance's new secretary general. Solana came to NATO at a crucial time for the alliance, just as it had begun its peacekeeping deployment to Bosnia after the Dayton Peace Accords. NATO had just completed its first major military operation, and had successfully brought the warring factions from the former Yugoslavia to the peace table. NATO was also in the second year of its Partnership for Peace program, and political momentum was building for expanding the alliance's membership. Although some analysts and past decision makers have already noted Solana's role in shaping NATO's post–Cold War transition, especially on the issue of expanding the alliance's membership at the July 1997 Madrid Summit, his leadership in NATO's history prior to and during NATO's war in Kosovo must also be understood.[1]

JAVIER SOLANA, 1995–1999

Javier Solana came to NATO with extensive experience in international diplomacy, although one would hardly predict such a

1. On Solana's leadership on NATO enlargement in Madrid, see Ronald D. Asmus, *Opening NATO's Door: How the Alliance Remade Itself for a New Era* (New York: Columbia University Press, 2002).

career based upon his previous professional experiences. Solana earned a Ph.D. in physics in 1968 from the University of Virginia, where he stayed to teach and do research until 1971, when he returned to Spain. Solana then joined the faculty at the Autonomous University of Madrid and then, in 1975, Complutense University. During this period, Solana compiled an extensive list of academic publications.

Upon his return to Spain, however, Solana became increasingly active in Spanish politics in the Spanish Socialist Worker's Party, and in 1977 he was elected to serve as a member of that party in the Spanish parliament. In 1982, as part of the Socialists' governing coalition, he became the minister of culture. More importantly, in 1992 Solana began his tenure as Spain's foreign minister, which lasted until his appointment as NATO secretary general in 1995. As Belgium did when Willy Claes served as its foreign minister, Spain also held the European Union's rotating presidency in the second half of 1995, while Solana was foreign minister. This experience broadened his diplomatic contacts and leadership opportunities across Europe, which later proved useful in leading the alliance. Somewhat ironically, given his future leadership of NATO, in 1982 Solana argued forcefully against Spain's membership in NATO and against the stationing of American military bases in Spain—viewing both NATO and the United States as too militaristic in their relations with the Soviet Union.

Much like those of his predecessors, the process of selecting Solana to become secretary general was contentious, and involved the traditional diplomatic bargaining among the allies over who was acceptable to everyone. Upon Claes's resignation announcement, the Netherlands forwarded its prime minister, Ruud Lubbers, who rapidly moved to the forefront as the leading candidate. However, Lubbers, who had secured British, French, and German support, was not acceptable to the United States, which allegedly felt that it had not been consulted properly on his candidacy. Journalistic reports at the time also suggested that Clinton administration officials were not impressed with Lubbers's knowledge of the security conditions surrounding events in Bosnia.[2]

2. Marlise Simons, "NATO Picks Spanish Foreign Minister for Secretary General," New York Times, December 2, 1995, A1; Rick Atkinson, "NATO Agrees

Lubbers's failed candidacy was followed by an American proposal of former Danish foreign minister Uffe Ellemann-Jensen. In response, France voiced its disapproval over Ellemann-Jensen's limited French-language skills and his opposition to France's nuclear-weapons tests that same year. Amidst these differences, Javier Solana rose to the top as the lead compromise candidate. Unlike those of Wörner and Claes, however, Solana's nomination generated some congressional opposition as well as newspaper-editorial criticism in the United States. Among the lead voices, Senators Jesse Helms (R-NC) and Bob Dole (R-KS) maintained that Solana's socialist credentials and his previous opposition to Spain's membership in NATO were two indications that the Clinton administration had erred grievously in supporting Solana.[3] The U.S. Congress, however, has no formal legislative role in the nomination process for the secretary general, and this criticism ended quickly upon Solana's formal installation as NATO's leader on December 19, 1995.

During his first two years as NATO's secretary general, Solana had developed the trust of the allies with his role in helping NATO expand its membership in 1997, which culminated at the Madrid Summit. He was also deeply involved in the negotiations that resulted in the NATO-Russia Founding Act in 1997. In the NATO-Russia Founding Act, these two former enemies came together to create a framework for enhancing dialogue across a host of issues, including peacekeeping, crisis management, conflict prevention, and conflict resolution. Solana was intimately involved in the negotiations between the United States and Russia, especially as a conduit for Deputy Secretary of State Strobe Talbott to the Russians in finding the needed diplomatic language that would allow for this new political arrangement, which lasted until Operation Allied Force, when the Russians left because of their opposition to NATO's air strikes. Solana proved to be a skilled diplomat and quite useful in these negotiations in 1997.

---

on Spaniard as Secretary General," *Washington Post*, December 2, 1995, A16; Bruce Clark, "Spanish Foreign Minister to Be New NATO Chief," *Financial Times*, December 2, 1995, 1.

3. See Atkinson, "NATO Agrees on Spaniard as Secretary General"; *Congressional Record* (December 6, 1995), H14139, H13941; and *Washington Times*, "Not the Best Choice for NATO," December 10, 1995, B2.

As described by a former Clinton State Department official, Ronald D. Asmus, Solana was also "a central figure in the endgame on NATO enlargement." As NATO began to consider the issue of alliance expansion, Solana exercised considerable leadership behind the scenes. In early 1997, Solana advised both Senator William Roth (R-DE) and Robert Hunter, U.S. ambassador to NATO, that many of the European allies were skeptical about alliance expansion if such a move would damage relations with Russia. Solana thus counseled that alliance expansion should not be discussed publicly at that time and that private meetings with the NATO allies should be the primary forum for any discussion of the issue.[4] His advice was largely accepted by the allies.

Through his private "confessionals" with each of the allies' ambassadors in the lead-up to the Madrid Summit, Solana also learned that wide differences of opinion existed within the alliance about potential new members. In an effort to raise a political warning that diplomatic work remained before consensus would be possible regarding which countries would be invited to join NATO, Solana aired these differences to the ambassadors three weeks before the start of the summit. Once the issue moved to the public agenda at the summit, the allies sought out Solana to find language satisfactory to all when debate ensued over the possible membership of the Baltic states, as well as Romania and Slovenia. The Czech Republic, Hungary, and Poland were all deemed acceptable candidates for membership, but France and, to a lesser extent, Italy led the effort in calling for the larger alliance expansion, focusing on the admission of Romania and Slovenia. After Solana was sought out to resolve these differences, he produced a draft communiqué on future membership that all the allies eventually approved. Thus, in both of these major decisions for the alliance, Solana became a quiet but critical negotiator for NATO, and in the process established himself as a skilled diplomat and certainly one whom the allies could trust.[5] These two major decisions for NATO in 1997, no doubt, enhanced Solana's leadership credentials prior to the Kosovo crisis.

When NATO and Solana faced the problems in Kosovo in March 1998, the crisis catapulted Solana into a new and different leader-

4. Asmus, *Opening NATO's Door*, 135 (quotation), 182, 348.
5. Ibid., 224, 247.

ship role for the alliance. The systemic political conditions that evolved in 1998 provided Solana with unique opportunities in NATO's history to shape policy on many of the alliance's political and military decisions for the war.

Systemic Conditions Facing Solana

Like all the previous secretaries general examined, Solana faced a host of conflicting systemic political conditions, which provided both limitations and opportunities to influence NATO's policies toward the Kosovo crisis in 1998 and 1999. It is first noteworthy that the Clinton administration and most Europeans recognized that President Slobodan Milosevic of Yugoslavia presented a real threat to regional stability in 1998. Because of his complicity with the Bosnian Serbs' military assault in Bosnia and Croatia in the early 1990s, and his support for brutal military tactics against the Kosovo Albanians in Yugoslavia, which began in March 1998, Milosevic's actions prompted a much quicker response from the allies than they ordinarily would have. Some within the Clinton administration, most notably Secretary of State Madeleine Albright, placed essentially all blame on Milosevic for Yugoslavia's ongoing problems and encouraged an expeditious military response. Unlike the diplomatic sentiments shared among the allies in the early 1990s, there was no notion of any political neutrality toward Milosevic. Although widespread international political sympathy did not necessarily exist for the Kosovo Liberation Army (KLA)—the rebel opposition group fighting for its independence from Milosevic in Kosovo—the Yugoslav president remained the target of most international criticism.[6]

At the same time, a second systemic political dynamic in 1998 was the fact of differing international views on how to address Milosevic's aggression. Although most states were willing to condemn

6. Ivo H. Daalder and Michael E. O'Hanlon, *Winning Ugly: NATO's War to Save Kosovo* (Washington, DC: Brookings Institution Press, 2000), 22–24. See also Eric Moskowitz and Jeffrey S. Lantis, "The War in Kosovo: Coercive Diplomacy," in *Contemporary Cases in U.S. Foreign Policy: From Terrorism to Trade,* ed. Ralph G. Carter (Washington, DC: Congressional Quarterly Press, 2001), 67.

Milosevic's repressive policies toward the Kosovo Albanians, the United Nations Security Council was divided on whether to authorize military action against Yugoslavia. The Russians and Chinese stood firm in their opposition to the use of force. Both states viewed Yugoslavia's problems as sovereign in nature, and thus a question best left for the country to resolve internally. In contrast, the United Kingdom and the United States appeared much more willing to threaten and potentially use force, with or without UN approval, although the Clinton administration still seemed interested in gaining some degree of multilateral approval for military action.[7]

The Serbian atrocities continued through the summer of 1998, and the United States and the United Kingdom went to the UN Security Council in September to seek its approval for enforcement action against Milosevic. The Western allies gained a strong condemnation of the Serbs' military actions in UN Security Council Resolution 1199, yet no formal approval for military strikes was specifically given. China and Russia included reservations in their votes, noting that additional authorization would be required before force could be used with UN backing. Arguably, these reservations could be considered "overkill," in that Resolution 1199 noted specifically that if the resolution's demands "to cease the violence" were not met, the Security Council would meet to "consider further action and additional measures to maintain or restore peace and stability in the region."[8] Although all states shared the view that Milosevic and the KLA must end their attacks, it was clear that profound differences remained at the United Nations over how best to address Milosevic. The Security Council's lukewarm response to Milosevic was the catalyst for a third systemic variable in 1998—the empowerment of NATO.

For a number of reasons, NATO became the hub of diplomatic activity in 1998. With the UN Security Council unwilling to approve use-of-force options to address Kosovo's growing humanitarian crisis, the United States and the United Kingdom moved aggressively to make NATO the principal multilateral decision-making body. Since Russia and China opposed military action, it was clear that a

7. Daalder and O'Hanlon, *Winning Ugly,* 43–44.
8. UN Security Council Resolution 1199, September 23, 1998; Craig Turner, "U.N. Vote Paves Way for Force in Kosovo," *Los Angeles Times,* September 24, 1998, A12. Namibia also voted against the use of force.

diplomatic route through the United Nations potentially meant that no enforcement action would ever take place. The United States' willingness to consider military force contrasted sharply with its indecisiveness from 1993 through the summer of 1995 over Bosnia.

One indicator of the United States' willingness to employ coercive diplomatic tactics came in June 1998, when NATO authorized military aircraft "fly-overs" of Serbian borders in the hopes of deterring Milosevic from additional human-rights violations in Kosovo.[9] The Clinton administration, led by Secretary of Defense William Cohen and Secretary of State Madeleine Albright, took an additional step and threatened direct military action against the Serbs if they did not cease their violence. Both Cohen and Albright maintained that international legal authority existed for strikes, even though neither the United Nations nor NATO had authorized such actions.[10] These statements caused consternation among some NATO allies, who responded with differing degrees of concern that UN Security Council authorization was needed before NATO could act on Milosevic. The negative European responses help explain the American and British efforts in September 1998 to return to the United Nations for another diplomatic solution.

Although some of the European allies still preferred UN Security Council endorsement of any forthcoming military action against Milosevic, NATO's stock had clearly risen since 1995 vis-à-vis the United Nations. The United Nations' dual-key arrangement with NATO that existed in 1993, 1994, and 1995 had been widely criticized, and UNPROFOR's poor legacy made it an easier decision in 1998 to eliminate the United Nations from playing any substantial military role.[11] NATO's (not the United Nations') sustained and

9. On Operation Determined Falcon, see Federation of American Scientists, http://www.globalsecurity.org/military/ops/determined_falcon.htm.

10. William Cohen, "News Briefing," June 11, 1998, U.S. Defense Department, http://www.defenselink.mil/news/Jun1998/to6111998 611nato.html; Madeleine K. Albright, "Press Conference at Lancaster House," June 12, 1998, U.S. State Department, http://secretary.state.gov/www/statements/1998/980612a.html.

11. Col. Robert C. Owen, ed., *Operation Deliberate Force: A Case Study in Effective Air Campaigning* (Maxwell Air Force Base, AL: Air University Press, 2000); senior NATO official "G," phone interview with author, July 10, 2004. See also Mark A. Bucknam, "The Influence of UN and NATO Theater-Level Commanders on the Use of Airpower over Bosnia during Deny Flight: 1993–1995" Ph.D. diss., King's College, 1999).

intensive two-week bombing campaign in 1995 had also succeeded in bringing all warring factions to the Dayton Peace Accords. Thus, the United Nations' widely perceived failures in Bosnia, coupled with an American willingness to work through NATO, resulted in a politically empowered alliance by autumn 1998.[12]

One final factor that had systemic relevance was Javier Solana himself. Although some doubts had existed initially over his ability to serve effectively as secretary general, in his first two years in office he proved himself an extremely adept diplomat and an effective leader of the alliance. As noted at the beginning of this chapter, Solana had already demonstrated that he could be a trusted and skilled diplomat, and he was a critical player at the 1997 Madrid Summit. Former secretary of state Madeleine Albright noted that Solana was a "master diplomat" on negotiations for the 1997 NATO-Russia Founding Act and was able to place pressure on Russia to agree to the charter under NATO's conditions. Much like Manfred Wörner's, Solana's credibility and stature at the alliance grew in his first years in office, earning him the trust and respect of the allies and later contributing to his political influence during Operation Allied Force, NATO's eventual bombing campaign in Kosovo.[13]

In facing these international political dynamics in 1998, prior to UN Security Council Resolution 1199, which came in September, Solana dealt with these systemic diplomatic challenges mostly behind the scenes. As the Serbs' military actions continued and heightened in the summer of 1998, Solana became increasingly alarmed that Milosevic was damaging NATO's credibility. Like Albright, Solana appeared ready to use force earlier than the rest of the allies and was calling privately for military action. In a September 1998 meeting with NATO defense ministers, Solana placed quiet pressure on NATO by sharing with the allies what a Serb general had told him: "A village a day keeps NATO away," which implied that as long as Milosevic moved slowly and cautiously through

12. John E. Peters, Stuart Johnson, Nora Bensahel, Timothy Liston, and Trac Williams, *European Contributions to Operation Allied Force* (Washington, DC RAND, 2001), 11.

13. Quotation from Madeleine Albright with Bill Woodward, *Madame Secretary* (New York: Mirimax Books, 2003), 256; senior U.S. Department of Defense official "A," interview with author in Brussels, June 1, 2001; senior NATO official "A," interview with author in Brussels, June 1, 2001.

Kosovo, the political momentum to curtail Yugoslavia's troops would not develop.[14]

Publicly, Solana was careful not to criticize any of the allies, and in general, he served as a public defender of NATO's policies at the time. Unlike Wörner, Solana placed no open pressure on the allies to act, but rather served as NATO's principal defender, threatening military action on Milosevic only in the most ambiguous and general terms, which essentially reflected alliance policy at the time.[15] Although Solana made some private efforts to change NATO's course, he made no public effort to steer NATO in a new direction.

The turning point for Solana's activism, influence, and systemic significance came with UN Security Council Resolution 1199. With respect to Solana's leadership in the alliance, the UN Security Council decision was important in two ways. First, after the resolution it could be argued that a United Nations diplomatic solution, which many of NATO's member states favored, had been attempted. Secondly, although Resolution 1199 called upon all warring factions to curtail their military maneuvers to avert a humanitarian catastrophe, the resolution failed to achieve military-authorization language akin to what had been gained for Bosnia, as well as for other enforcement actions that the United Nations had authorized in the 1990s. The political result was that the UN Security Council demonstrated its weak resolve and in effect removed itself from the political debate. The United States and Britain then shifted their primary diplomatic activities to NATO. This considerable systemic change, which made the security scene quite different from that in the situation of either Manfred Wörner or Willy Claes, brought the secretary general heightened political influence at NATO, as the North Atlantic Council became the principal diplomatic forum for resolving the conflict. Thus, although Solana was calling privately for systemic change because of NATO's and the United Nations' failure to address the Balkan violence in 1998, it was the change in systemic

14. Quotation in Barton Gellman, "The Path to Crisis: How the United States and Its Allies Went to War," *Washington Post*, April 18, 1999, A1; Moskowitz and Lantis, "The War in Kosovo," 67.

15. See Javier Solana, "NATO and European Security in the Twenty-first Century," May 13, 1998, NATO, http://www.nato.int/docu/speech/1998/s98051a.htm, and "Remarks to the Press," May 28, 1998, NATO, http://www.nato.int/docu/speech/1998/s980528a.htm.

conditions that led to Solana's organizational empowerment in the North Atlantic Council.

Organizational Leadership

The systemic conditions surrounding Javier Solana in 1998, in many respects, created unique organizational leadership opportunities for him in the NAC. It should be recognized, however, that there was no guarantee that Solana would succeed in leading the NAC on the Kosovo crisis. Much evidence suggests that he played a profoundly important role across a host of issues facing NATO and its policies toward Milosevic.

On his general leadership style as NAC chairman, many viewed Solana as an individual with a tremendous political presence. To all the allies, Solana was approachable, he never embarrassed diplomats from member delegations in public, and he possessed the empirically intangible but real personal quality of being a consensus builder when trying to maintain cohesion among strong political personalities. When disagreements arose, in the vast majority of cases Solana handled them behind closed doors, which helped preserve his ability to mediate differences and prevent controversies from becoming divisive. Senior officials at NATO viewed Solana as an "honest broker." This view is supported in the memoirs of former SACEUR General Wesley Clark, who notes that Solana brought out the concerns of *all* allies during the eventual bombing campaign, including the views of small states such as Belgium and Luxembourg.[16] Other key decision makers involved in Operation Allied Force have openly commended Solana for his consensus-building skills as NAC chairman.[17] In the aftermath of Allied Force, it was widely felt at NATO headquarters that the campaign was a "NATO" operation, and not strictly an "American" mission, a feeling that was partly due to Solana's ability to listen to and convey all the allies' concerns.

16. Former NATO deputy permanent representative "A," interview with author in Brussels, June 5, 2001; Craig R. Whitney, "Crisis in the Balkans: Man in the News," *New York Times,* April 1, 1999, A15; General Wesley K. Clark, *Waging Modern War* (New York: Public Affairs, 2001), 339.

17. Klaus Nauman, "U.S. Policy on NATO Military Operations in Kosovo," *United States Senate, Armed Services Committee,* November 3, 1999, 458.

When opposition would arise in the NAC, another diplomatic tool Solana would employ, much like Wörner, was to "go above" the NATO ambassadors and persuade their more senior governmental officials to cooperate with NATO. When NATO ambassadors became too aggressive in their opposition to Allied Force, Solana would phone their heads of state to place additional pressure on them to comply with NATO's mission. In his previous role as Spain's foreign minister, Solana had developed a thick diplomatic "Rolodex" to many of Europe's foreign policy elite. Solana would often not tell the ambassador that he was using such means, but it would soon become clear that Solana's diplomatic contacts were deep, which would result in bringing NATO ambassadors "into line" when disagreements arose.[18] Similar to Manfred Wörner's long list of personal relationships and friends in government, Solana's contacts had little to do with the formal position of secretary general, but were instead based on his years of experience in foreign policy making.

On one occasion, about halfway through Operation Allied Force, when some officials of the Czech Republic actively and aggressively criticized the bombing campaign, Solana gave the Czech Republic's ambassador to NATO, Karel Kovanda, a rather fierce scolding for the opposition voices coming from his country. Solana allegedly impressed upon Kovanda the importance of alliance unity—especially for the Czech Republic, which had been a full member of NATO for only approximately one month.[19] Although Wörner and Claes were very willing to confront NATO ambassadors during tense moments, such a bold action toward an ambassador was out of the norm for Solana and was not reflective of his usual organizational leadership approach. Given that the exchange was reported by the *Washington Post* and was almost completely unrepresentative of Solana's leadership style (in terms of both his temperament and the public manner in which it occurred), Solana was likely trying either to appease alliance members who were growing unhappy with the Czech Republic or to

18. Karel Kovanda, Czech Republic ambassador to NATO, interview with author in Brussels, June 5, 2001; NATO ambassador "A," interview with author in Brussels, June 5, 2001; senior NATO official "D," interview with author in Brussels, June 1, 2001.

19. William Drozdiak, "NATO's Newcomers Are Shaken by Airstrikes; Czechs, Hungarians Express Greatest Dismay," *Washington Post*, April 12, 1999, A17.

place diplomatic pressure on any NATO member who was threatening alliance unity during the war, or both.

Solana's leadership of the NAC did not prevent him from maintaining close diplomatic contact and sustained dialogue with UN Secretary General Kofi Annan during the bombing campaign. Although this relationship was not widely reported on, it was appreciated by some governments because it demonstrated Solana's respect for those allies whose views remained mixed on the use of force without UN Security Council approval.[20]

Solana's leadership and influence in the NAC were also assisted by his untiring and widely recognized work ethic. It was not rare during the bombing campaign for Solana to phone members of his staff at any hour of the day or night to share ideas or to initiate new policy. While ambitious politicians of all nationalities often work long hours, Solana's work ethic was viewed as near compulsion by many at NATO and left no doubt about his commitment to NATO's success and unity.[21] Although Wörner and Claes are similarly remembered for their dedication and work ethic, among his colleagues Solana's "workaholic tendencies" were a frequently noted personal quality and were considered a factor in his influence within the NAC.

Solana ran NAC meetings very differently than Wörner or Claes had. The meetings during his tenure were more open and free, and sometimes ambiguous, leaving some senior American military officials wondering at times whether any decision had been reached.[22] Solana was not openly confrontational with ambassadors who disagreed with him, and he was more willing to allow debate and discussions to run their course. This diplomatic tactic was eventually helpful in a number of ways, both prior to Operation Allied Force and during actual combat.

In the aftermath of UN Security Council Resolution 1199, with heightened interest from the United States and the United Kingdom in gaining NATO authorization to threaten military action against Milosevic, Solana was still faced with a number of European allies

---

20. NATO deputy permanent representative "B," interview with author in Brussels, May 31, 2001.

21. Senior NATO official "A" interview, June 1, 2001; senior NATO official "E," interview with author in Brussels, June 5, 2001.

22. Senior U.S. Department of Defense official "A" interview, June 1, 2001; senior NATO official "E" interview, June 5, 2001.

who remained wary over NATO's legal authority to act without specific UN authorization. Those allies who remained most concerned were Belgium, Germany, Greece, Italy, Spain, and, to a lesser extent, France.[23] International legal analysts maintain that when the United Nations Charter was written, its framers' intent was clear: that regional organizations could act independently of the UN Security Council in self-defense. Article 51 of the United Nations Charter, which permits member states to act in their own self-defense, was written primarily as a response to the demands of South American members who wanted to ensure the right of regional organizations to act in their own self-defense if they were ever attacked.[24] In addition, Article 52 of the UN Charter states that regional organizations may use force, as long as "their activities are consistent with the purposes and principles of the United Nations." Yet differences of opinion remained in the alliance in the summer and early fall of 1998 over whether NATO could act absent UN approval. In light of these divisions, with American and British approval, Solana began to seek from the allies an Activation Order (ACTORD), which would allow NATO to begin preparations for a military strike if necessary. Such a NAC decision would be a signal of NATO's commitment to meet the threat and would set the process of using force, if necessary, in motion.

Strong reservations about the use of force persisted at NATO headquarters though late September and into early October 1998. In the end, however, Solana was credited with crafting a legal position for the alliance that allowed for the ACTORD decision. After a little more than two weeks of debate, on October 10, 1998, Solana announced that all allies agreed that "sufficient legal basis" existed for NATO military planning. Three days later, the NATO ambassadors endorsed the ACTORD and gave the secretary general authority to initiate limited air strikes in a phased aerial assault if a diplomatic resolution was not achieved.[25]

23. Catherine Guicherd, "International Law and the War in Kosovo," *Survival* 41, no. 2 (1999): 19–34.

24. Joseph L. Kunz, "Privileges and Immunities of International Organizations," *American Journal of International Law* 41, no. 4 (1947): 828–73.

25. Daalder and O'Hanlon, *Winning Ugly*, 45; Javier Solana, "Statement to the Press by the Secretary General following Decision on the ACTORD," October 13, 1998, NATO, http://www.nato.int/docu/speech/1998/s981013a.htm.

Solana's diplomatic achievement within the NAC resulted from his ability to find consensus using the semantic ambiguity of the phrase "sufficient legal basis." This terminology allowed the members of the alliance to justify to their varied domestic constituencies NATO's international legal authority to act—although Solana avoided precise language within the NAC. Members could make different appeals; they could cite "UN norms," the appropriate historical intent and role for the UN Security Council, or even the Security Council's vote in September to appeal to domestic audiences, which varied widely across the alliance. In his lobbying efforts, Solana himself relied upon UN Security Council Resolution 1199, the Serbs' unwillingness to comply with these demands, the threat of a humanitarian catastrophe, and the deteriorating conditions in Kosovo.[26]

In his efforts to find consensus, Solana consulted widely with all members of the alliance. Rather than stressing the differences among the allies, which were considerable in the immediate aftermath of Security Council Resolution 1199, Solana stressed the areas of agreement, which were enough to gain the NAC's approval to begin preparations for military strikes. Solana's background as a Socialist foreign minister from Spain and his activism against NATO earlier in his political career may have been useful in building support among some of the European allies who were more hesitant to support use-of-force options.[27] No doubt, Solana benefited from the United States' and the United Kingdom's backing, but interviews with lead participants as well as journalistic coverage of these events show Solana as the principal architect of NATO's legal claims.[28] Solana succeeded, then, in finding common legal ground for NATO military action without UN approval, capitalizing on the ambiguous legal term he identified within the NAC.

26. See Guicherd, "International Law and the War in Kosovo," 27–28, and Javier Solana, "Statement to the Press by NATO Secretary General Solana," October 27, 1998, NATO, http://www.nato.int/docu/speech/1998/s981027a.htm.

27. John E. Peters et al., *European Contributions to Operation Allied Force*, 13; Robert Kupiecki, deputy permanent representative to NATO from Poland, interview with author in Brussels, June 5, 2001; U.S. State Department official "A" interview, June 5, 2001; senior NATO official "B," interview with author in Brussels, May 31, 2001.

28. William Drozdiak, "Allies Grim, Milosevic Defiant Amid Kosovo Uncertainty," *Washington Post,* October 8, 1998, A27.

When NATO later moved toward possible military action before the diplomatic efforts with Yugoslavia in Rambouillet, France, in January 1999, and in the days immediately before Operation Allied Force in March 1999, no substantive legal debate ensued within the alliance over its authority to conduct air strikes. Although debate on NATO's authority to use force continued in legal circles and within the domestic constituencies of some NATO allies, Solana had won the debate in Brussels in October 1998.[29] Solana's efforts at this time set the legal foundation for NATO's bombing campaign in March 1999, when international legal questions were no longer on NATO's agenda.

Solana's ability to find consensus was one of his major achievements as secretary general. Admittedly, Solana was allowed to go forward with this position by the allies, with strong support from the United States and the United Kingdom. His achievement also came when NATO's credibility was being questioned as Milosevic continued with his atrocities. Moreover, the allies and Manfred Wörner had also done the difficult work at the 1991 Rome Summit of transforming NATO's post–Cold War role to potentially include the sorts of missions that Solana and NATO's major powers were considering for the Kosovo crisis. Yet many at NATO credit the "sufficient legal basis" decision to Solana's personal ability to craft this position.

Another important element of Solana's NAC leadership was his willingness to place his position and office personally at the epicenter of the decision-making process. When the NAC reached its AC-TORD decision on October 13, 1998, Solana announced the NAC's authorization to begin preparations for a military operation in ninety-six hours if a diplomatic solution to the crisis was not achieved.[30] Solana then traveled to Belgrade, along with SACEUR General Wesley Clark and Chairman of the Military Committee

29. For example, see Christine Chinkin, "Kosovo: A 'Good' or 'Bad' War?" *American Journal of International Law* 93, no. 4 (1999): 841–47; Jonathan I. Charney, "Anticipatory Humanitarian Intervention in Kosovo," *American Journal of International Law* 93, no. 4 (1999): 834–41; and Richard A. Falk, "Kosovo, World Order, and the Future of International Law," *American Journal of International Law* 93, no. 4 (1999): 847–57.

30. Solana, "Statement to the Press by the Secretary General following Decision on the ACTORD."

General Klaus Nauman, to deliver the message to Milosevic that NATO was ready to use force if necessary.[31] With NATO now at the center of diplomatic action, Solana became one of the chief diplomats for the alliance and a lead voice in Belgrade in discussing the ACTORD with Milosevic.[32]

Similarly, before the meetings at Rambouillet, France, on January 30, 1999, when the Kosovar representatives and the Yugoslav government agreed to meet for diplomatic talks to discuss the fighting, the NAC again provided the secretary general with, prima facie, some discretion in determining whether force would be used. In its official press statement, the NAC noted, "The Council has therefore agreed today that the NATO Secretary General may authorise air strikes against targets on FRY [Federal Republic of Yugoslavia] territory. The NATO Secretary General will take full account of the position and actions of the Kosovar leadership and all Kosovar armed elements in and around Kosovo in reaching his decision on military action."[33] Such a decision contrasts sharply with NAC decisions to authorize military action in 1994, when the council did not elevate the secretary general, even as a figurehead, to the position of decision maker with any discretionary authority. In the hours prior to the initiation of Operation Allied Force, Solana told the press, "I have just directed SACEUR, General Clark, to initiate air operations in the Federal Republic of Yugoslavia. I have taken this decision after extensive consultations in recent days with all the Allies, and after it became clear that the final diplomatic effort of Ambassador Holbrooke in Belgrade has not met with success."[34]

These press statements and NAC decisions provide additional insight into Solana's role in leading the alliance and his level of power in the NAC. The NAC's decisions placed Solana at NATO's epicen-

31. Javier Solana, "Press Points by Secretary General, Dr. Javier Solana," October 15, 1998, NATO, http://www.nato.int/docu/speech/1998/s981015a.htm.
32. Clark, *Waging Modern War*, 145–47.
33. NATO Press Release (99)12, "Statement by the North Atlantic Council on Kosovo," January 30, 1999, NATO, http://www.nato.int/docu/pr/1999/p99-012e.htm.
34. NATO Press Release (99)40, "Press Statement by Dr. Javier Solana, Secretary General of NATO, on Decision to Initiate Air Operations over Federal Republic of Yugoslavia," March 23, 1999, NATO, http://www.nato.int/docu/pr/1999/p99-040e.htm.

ter, which made him a real player and diplomatic messenger regarding the decision to use force. Admittedly, Solana would have been unable to call for military strikes if support had not existed in the alliance. Yet at the same time, the resolution language associated with the ACTORD decision, the Rambouillet meetings, and the NAC's final threats aimed at Milosevic in the hours before the initiation of Operation Allied Force suggests an empowerment of the secretary general that has no parallel in NATO's history. In part, this language was due to the United States' strong preference for having the operation viewed internationally as a NATO operation. In shifting attention to Europe, the Clinton administration made a clear choice to signal that this was a NATO operation, which, by definition, had Europe's backing.

The Clinton administration also wanted all press attention to focus on NATO's political headquarters in Brussels, rather than its military headquarters in Mons, Belgium.[35] When the bombing operation began, SACEUR Wesley Clark had his staff phone the National Broadcasting Network (NBC), whose initial reports had announced that the *United States* had begun to bomb in Kosovo. Clark's staff provided NBC with information to demonstrate that the campaign was a NATO operation and should not be termed an "American" military action.[36] Thus, with American foreign policy so explicitly favorable to NATO, Solana's role became heightened.

Moreover, in March 1999, President Clinton had also just survived the U.S. Congress's impeachment efforts. Under such difficult domestic political conditions, it was politically easier to engage in military action with NATO's full backing. With NATO support, the Clinton administration would be immune to criticism that its military actions were diversionary in intent. The criticism that Clinton was using the military to potentially improve upon his damaged political credibility simply had no credence since the NATO allies were full partners in the bombing.

Many of the European allies also had political incentives to empower NATO's secretary general. First, a NATO operation was by

35. Senior U.S. Department of Defense official "A" interview, June 1, 2001; senior NATO official "A" interview, June 1, 2001. See also Clark, *Waging Modern War*, 186.

36. Clark, *Waging Modern War*, 195.

definition multilateral, and thus not the United States acting alone. By conducting the military operation through the alliance, the European allies would have a say in determining how the operation progressed and was conducted. American power would be checked, and this was politically useful to states that harbored some anti-American sentiment, or general opposition to military action. Second, although Solana had no de facto authority to require the alliance to take military action, the appearance of such a framework was certainly beneficial to some of the allies. In states where domestic opposition to military action was more intense, the NAC decision to seemingly empower the secretary general gave the appearance of transferring the final decision to go to war to the secretary general. In some states, especially Germany, Greece, and Italy, the domestic opposition to Allied Force and the concern for civilian casualties were considerable.[37] Through the language employed, some governments could avoid the appearance of a formal vote on military action.[38] Although the reality was different, in that Solana was not making the final decision for the allies, the resolution language gave some "political cover" to the European governments who faced considerable domestic opposition.

In early April, when Operation Allied Force progressed and the allies moved past Phase I and II targets and into the more intense "Phase III" of the campaign, which included strikes in and around Belgrade, Solana was given, and to some degree asserted, additional decision-making discretion in the NAC over the types of targets that could be hit.[39] In describing these events, General Klaus Nauman, the chairman of NATO's Military Committee, later recounted, "We realized that we would never get another formal decision of the NATO Council to escalate to phase three, which after all, had meant an all-out war against Yugoslavia. So the Chairman of the NATO Council, Secretary General Solana, chose the procedure to tell the council, 'I, as secretary general, interpret the—our discussion in that and that way, and I hope that you can go along

37. Pierre Martin and Mark R. Brawley, eds., *Alliance Politics, Kosovo, and NATO's War: Allied Force or Forced Allies?* (New York: Palgrave, 2000).

38. Robert Kupiecki, deputy permanent representative to NATO from Poland, interview with author in Brussels, May 31, 2001; John Norris, *Collision Course: NATO, Russia, and Kosovo* (Westport, CT: Praeger, 2005), 60.

39. Daalder and O'Hanlon, *Winning Ugly*, 118.

with that.' So it was stated."[40] Again, through Solana's ambiguous decision-making approach exercised in the NAC, which alliance members could accept, Solana then directed the SACEUR into Phase III bombings with no explicit, but rather tacit, approval from the NAC.

Again, one reason for empowering Solana within the NAC on the Phase III military strikes was the need to insulate and protect member states from domestic criticism. By making Solana the ostensible "final" decision maker for the use of force, states in the alliance would not have to publicly defend the specific bombing targets. By giving Solana the political responsibility for Allied Force, member states whose domestic critics were louder than others could shift the attention to Solana (and to the United States as NATO's primary military implementor) for any mistakes that might have taken place once the operation began.[41] Thus, the authority that Solana was given and then eventually used during the military campaign served the interests of many within the alliance.

Once the bombings began, Solana used additional NAC decision-making procedures that simultaneously empowered him while again protecting the NATO allies. For example, about two months into Allied Force, Solana announced that approximately twenty thousand additional soldiers would be sent to the region, and that "all options remain open" regarding the use of these ground troops. Upon this announcement, Solana invoked the "silence procedure," which stipulates that a resolution will automatically be passed by the NAC after a stated time period set by the secretary general unless a member state objects.[42] The silence procedure is only exercised by the secretary general, but it is used with the backing of most states in the alliance.

This decision-making tactic can be useful in that it forces a less-enthusiastic ally to formally oppose the secretary general. Such opposition can be expressed privately, but in the event of strong opposition, the opposing ally could go public with its disapproval for

40. Nauman, quoted in Peters et al., *European Contributions to Operation Allied Force*, 27.

41. NATO deputy permanent representative "B" interview, May 31, 2001; Norris, *Collision Course*, 60.

42. William Drozdiak, "Deployment of New Ground Forces Adds Pressure within Alliance," *International Herald Tribune*, May 26, 1999, 10.

the proposed action. Public disagreement would place NATO member states in a conflict for the world press to consume, and in 1999, this would have been news that Milosevic would welcome. The decision to "break silence" would demonstrate profound disagreement with alliance policy, and would make a certain state or group of states "spoilers" at NATO.[43] Given the intense media scrutiny that NATO faced at the time, and the challenge to NATO's military credibility because of the ongoing bombing campaign, it would have been very difficult for a state to remain private in breaking the silence. Such conditions presented Solana with a favorable political environment for invoking the procedure—and this proved to be a successful leadership tactic, as silence continued and the military threat to Milosevic intensified.

At the same time, it must be understood that the silence procedure also allows states *not* to take positions publicly, which can again serve to insulate them from their domestic critics. As has already been illustrated, a number of the European allies were quite concerned about domestic political repercussions from the military action, so the silence procedure was a good tactic to employ so that members could remain silent as NATO moved forward. Solana's decision to use this procedure is another example of his effective consensus-building skills within the NAC.

One final illustration of Solana's leadership as NAC chairman stems from his excellent relations with the Clinton administration. While earning his doctorate at the University of Virginia, Solana had become familiar with American politics. During his days as Spain's foreign minister, he had also been friends with Secretary of State Warren Christopher, and thus he had already developed good ties with the Clinton administration.[44]

When the NATO ambassadors met in Washington for the alliance's fiftieth anniversary in April 1999, with Operation Allied Force seemingly making little military progress, President Clinton indicated to the press that he supported *Solana's* interest in begin-

43. See Paul Gallis, "NATO's Decision-Making Procedure," *Congressional Research Service Report for Congress*, RS21510, May 5, 2003; and Leo G. Michel, "NATO Decisionmaking: Au Revoir to the Consensus Rule?" *Strategic Forum* 202 (March 2004), http://www.ndu.edu/inss/strforum/SF202/sf202.htm.

44. Senior NATO official "A" interview, June 1, 2001; senior U.S. Department of Defense official "A" interview, June 1, 2001.

ning an assessment of a ground-troop option for the operation.[45] Although the United States still played the lead role in directing military operations for the alliance, Clinton's "deference" to Solana suggested that the secretary general would have an independent impact on NATO's operational approach and direction. Clinton's public display of deference was likely done to ward off European criticism that the bombings were dominated by the United States. In allowing Solana to introduce the ground-troop option, the Clinton administration would also not be the lead voice in introducing a new military approach—one that it had removed from all consideration at the initiation of the conflict. Solana himself did have an interest in pursuing a ground-troop option at this stage of the military campaign, but whatever Clinton's specific reasoning, the political result was that Solana's voice would carry additional weight in the alliance. At minimum, Clinton's deference suggested considerable trust in Solana and American confidence in his leadership of the NAC.[46]

Thus, through an array of means, Solana exercised tremendous political power within the NAC. Because of his own exceptional diplomatic skills and trust earned over time, his ability to find consensus through different diplomatic tactics, and the particular set of political conditions that varied across NATO's member states at the time, Solana became a critical player within the NAC. His relationship with the SACEUR provides similar examples of instrumental leadership roles during the bombing campaign.

45. Bill Clinton, "Remarks following Discussions with NATO Secretary General Javier Solana and Exchange with Reporters," *Weekly Compilation of Presidential Documents* 35 (May 3, 1999): 705. It is significant that Clinton singled out Solana among NATO leaders.

46. John M. Broder, "Crisis in the Balkans: The White House; On Groups Troops Issue, Clinton Takes Back Seat," *New York Times*, April 24, 1999, A7; Dana Priest, "Kosovo Land Threat May Have Won War," *Washington Post*, September 19, 1999, A1; senior NATO official "B" interview, May 31, 2001. See Barton Gellman, "The Path to Crisis: How the United States and Its Allies Went to War," *Washington Post*, April 18, 1999, A1, on American leadership of the alliance.

Working with the SACEUR: Solana and Wesley Clark

Another key element in Solana's efforts to build and keep alliance consensus was his relationship with NATO's military commander, SACEUR General Wesley K. Clark. As already demonstrated, the relationship between NATO's political leader and the SACEUR can potentially provide much insight into the secretary general's ability to influence military decisions at NATO. Solana came to NATO with much less military expertise than Manfred Wörner, yet his limited background did not prevent him from playing a critical role in shaping military decisions for the alliance.[47] Much evidence demonstrates that through his relationship with Clark, Solana was instrumental in shaping NATO's seventy-eight-day bombing campaign against Milosevic and his Serb troops.

When NATO authorized the use of force in October 1998, and later initiated Operation Allied Force, on March 24, 1999, the NAC authorized the secretary general to take military action against the Yugoslav government according to three bombing phases. Phase I included military strikes on Serbian air-defense systems and any troops in Kosovo. Phase II included what General Clark referred to as the "Limited Air Operation." This phase allowed for strikes on ground forces, headquarters, and other military outposts below the 44th parallel in Yugoslavia. Phase III targets permitted strikes in and around Belgrade, where the risk of civilian casualties was most controversial. Allied Force began with Phase I targets on March 24, 1999, and by day four Clark was permitted to strike Phase II targets. By day nine, Clark began bombing Phase III targets upon consultation with Solana.[48]

Although Solana exercised broad political authority in overseeing the operation, the decision-making reality was that the major powers (France, Germany, Italy, the United Kingdom, and most importantly the United States) had substantial input to the SACEUR in determining what targets would be hit. General Clark notes that besides working with NATO officials to determine bombing targets

47. Senior NATO official "C," interview with author in Brussels, May 31 2001.

48. Benjamin Lambeth, *NATO's Air War for Kosovo* (Washington, DC: RAND 2001), 28–29. See also Clark, *Waging Modern War*, 176, 219.

his selected targets were also cleared by the United States Joint Chiefs of Staff and senior officials at the White House.[49] Solana's job, like Clark's, was to ensure that NATO succeeded in its military efforts and that diplomatic unity continued among the nineteen allies during the military campaign. Close dialogue between Solana, who was in Brussels, and Clark, who was in Mons, Belgium, at NATO's Supreme Headquarters Allied Powers Europe (SHAPE), would be key for ensuring military success and diplomatic unity.

Over the seventy-eight-day course of Allied Force, much evidence suggests that Solana and Clark worked extremely well together. When Solana sensed reservations or outright opposition to Clark's proposed targets, he relayed these sentiments back to the SACEUR. When internal opposition in the alliance increased to politically threatening levels, Solana requested Clark's presence at NATO headquarters in Brussels and encouraged him to meet privately with NATO ambassadors. In effect, Solana became an advocate for Clark, who faced strenuous if not unrealistic demands from some members of the alliance who wanted to conduct a war but refused to take casualties, make mistakes, or contribute in any way to the deaths of civilians. Solana was particularly useful to Clark in helping the SACEUR build support for the more sensitive strikes that faced opposition in the alliance. Solana also was able to place pressure on the allies when they began to waiver in their support for Allied Force, and thus he served as a lobbyist for the SACEUR.[50]

Solana was attuned to the political sensitivities within the alliance as to how much military force the allies were ready to use. From early on in the campaign, behind the scenes, Clark wanted a ground-troop option, which had been publicly eliminated at the initiation of the bombings by the United States and others in the alliance. In an effort to contain Clark's enthusiasm for ground troops,

49. Steven Lee Meyers, "All in Favor of This Target, Say Yes, Si, Oui, Ja," *New York Times,* April 25, 1999, A4; Dana Priest, "France Played Skeptic on Kosovo Attacks," *Washington Post,* September 20, 1999, A1; Clark, *Waging Modern War,* 78.

50. Clark, *Waging Modern War,* 177; Michael Ignatieff, *Virtual War: Kosovo and Beyond* (New York: Picador, 2000), 102; senior NATO official "A" interview, June 1, 2001; Priest, "France Played Skeptic," A1. Former president Bill Clinton also suggests an effective working relationship between Solana and Clark (Bill Clinton, *My Life* [New York: Alfred A. Knopf, 2004], 858).

Solana advised the SACEUR not to push aggressively or openly for them, which would threaten alliance cohesion. Clark eventually recognized that Solana's advice was the best route to follow politically, and he heeded Solana's recommendation.[51]

To some degree during Allied Force, Solana also kept Clark attuned to politics being played out in Washington, DC. Solana's close connection to senior Clinton officials was especially important given that the SACEUR did not have the full backing of the Department of Defense or, at times, even of senior officials at the White House. In contrast, Solana had frequent access to the White House.[52] Somewhat ironically for the American SACEUR, it was the Spanish secretary general who told him that his presence was not welcomed at NATO's summit in April 1999 in Washington, DC, during the midst of the bombing campaign. At the same time, some evidence also indicates that Solana feared that Clark was still too assertive on the issue of ground troops and so sought to have Clark's influence at the Washington Summit constrained.[53] This aspect of Solana's relations with Clark is difficult to capture precisely, but evidence indicates that Solana used his contacts with senior American official both to inform Clark of political developments in Washington and to ward off problems that Solana felt Clark would cause among the allies.

On occasion, Solana also vetoed target requests from Clark in response to heavy criticism from certain NATO members. Although Solana's "vetoes" were exercised infrequently, one senior NATO official noted that on a number of occasions Solana vetoed Clark's requests to hit the Yugoslav television outlets, which help explain why NATO repeatedly struck oil refineries even though they had little strategic value to the Serbs.[54] Solana's authority also extended to SHAPE's media relations, which arguably should fall under the SACEUR's jurisdiction. On one occasion during Allied Force, when Solana disapproved of how one of Clark's spokesmen conducted his communication duties, Solana required

51. Moskowitz and Lantis, "The War in Kosovo," 80–81; Clark, *Waging Modern War*, 15, 166.

52. Clark, *Waging Modern War*, 262. Solana was also in frequent contact with National Security Advisor Sandy Berger (senior NATO official "A" interview June 1, 2001).

53. Norris, *Collision Course*, 49–53.

54. Senior NATO official "A" interview, June 1, 2001.

Clark to remove the individual for what Solana viewed as inept relations with the press.[55]

In terms of Solana's and Clark's ideological dispositions toward the problems in Kosovo and NATO's post–Cold War evolution, all evidence suggests that they shared similar views. As illustrated by Solana's calls for NATO to confront Milosevic as early as September 1998, and by statements in Clark's memoirs, both saw the conflict in Kosovo as one that threatened NATO's credibility and presented a moral outrage to Europe. The secretary general and the SACEUR did not have to struggle over the appropriate role for the alliance in the Balkans or in its wider evolution in European security affairs; their likemindedness facilitated cooperation between these central leaders at NATO.[56]

In sum, the ideological similarities between the SACEUR and the secretary general, Solana's well-informed understanding of the allies' military preferences, and the NAC's decision to allow Solana a crucial role in moving the alliance into different bombing phases all enhanced Solana's influence vis-à-vis the SACEUR during Operation Allied Force. Although the final bombing decisions remained with the major powers in the alliance (principally the United States), it is clear that the SACEUR relied extensively upon Solana during the bombing campaign.[57] When compared to the relationships between SACEURs and secretaries general in the Cold War era, when SACEURs such as Dwight Eisenhower and Lauris Norstad dominated NATO decision making, these findings stand in strong contrast. In this case, Solana and Clark stood more as equals, striving to win the war while maintaining alliance unity.

Conclusion

When Javier Solana began his term as NATO's ninth secretary general, it would have been difficult to predict the leadership role

55. Clark, *Waging Modern War*, 249.
56. Ibid., 134; Alexander Nicholl and Lionel Barber, "Diplomat at War: Man in the News Javier Solana," *Financial Times*, May 15, 1999, 10; senior U.S. Department of Defense official "A" interview, June 1, 2001; NATO ambassador "A" interview, June 5, 2001; senior NATO official "A" interview, June 1, 2001.
57. Dana Priest, "United Front Was Divided Within," *Washington Post*, September 21, 1999, A1.

that he would eventually play both leading up to and during Opera
tion Allied Force. Solana became NATO's leader as a compromise
candidate, with some Americans questioning his Socialist Party af
filiation. Although Manfred Wörner and, to a lesser extent, Will
Claes had both asserted leadership roles at NATO that were uncom
mon for secretaries general, there was no guarantee that Solana
would similarly prove instrumental in shaping NATO's ongoing
evolution. After his departure to become the European Union's high
representative for common foreign and security policy in Octobe
1999, however, much evidence now indicates that Solana played
historic role in helping NATO defeat Milosevic and, more generally
in promoting transatlantic unity during a critical period in NATO'
evolution.

Much of Solana's ability to lead NATO stemmed from the systemi
political conditions in 1998, which provided the secretary genera
with truly unique leadership opportunities. Unlike Manfred Wörne
and Willy Claes, Solana was presented with an especially favorabl
political environment for leadership at NATO, including strong sup
port from the Clinton administration coupled with the wider recog
nition that Milosevic's brutal policies could not be tolerated agair
The United Nations' poor peacekeeping performance in Bosnia in th
first half of the 1990s and the UN Security Council's unwillingness t
endorse military action in 1998 shifted the diplomatic center of actior
to Brussels. Before UN Security Council Resolution 1199, Solana die
not publicly challenge the actions of any alliance members, and in
stead, in a fashion somewhat similar to Willy Claes's method, re
served most of his lobbying for policy change to private settings witl
NATO representatives. Yet after the UN Security Council failed t
yield a decision for military action and as the diplomatic momentun
shifted to Brussels, Solana moved aggressively to make NATO th
lead multilateral enforcement body to prevent additional atrocities ii
Kosovo. Solana eventually helped produce systemic changes in hov
Kosovo would be addressed, but his efforts came through his leadei
ship role as NAC chairman—as the systemic political conditions fa
vored a transatlantic solution to the crisis.

Within the North Atlantic Council, Solana exercised a leadershij
approach that was very different from his predecessors'. Wörne
and especially Claes are remembered for their occasionally as
sertive leadership styles, in which they reprimanded ambassador
and openly inserted their own policy perspectives. Solana was mor

passive in the NAC and is remembered for his consistent congeniality and, at times, more laissez-faire oversight of NAC discussions. Although not all member states appreciated his style of diplomacy, in his case it proved to be an effective method for identifying consensus positions and keeping the alliance unified during the bombing campaign. Given the mixed public opinion across Europe on NATO's bombing, Solana was able to exercise leadership in the NAC by placing himself, in the view of the public, at the center of NAC decisions. His ability to find "sufficient legal basis" for military action against Milosevic, absent UN Security Council approval, and his leadership of the NAC as NATO tacitly approved of Phase III military targets stand out as critical and historic actions during his tenure. His workaholic tendencies, his strong support from the United States, the personal trust he had cultivated, and his extensive list of political friendships across Europe were other factors that certainly contributed to his successful leadership of the NAC.

Solana's partnership with SACEUR Wesley Clark was another critical element of his leadership at NATO. Solana and Clark's shared belief that Milosevic must be stopped and the close coordination that the two maintained during Allied Force certainly helped sustain transatlantic unity over the difficult two and a half months of air strikes. As Willy Claes and George Joulwan had, Solana and Clark proved to have an effective partnership during the military campaign. Although Clark maintained overall control of military strategy and tactical decisions, much evidence suggests that Solana's voice was influential in shaping military decisions during the campaign. Such influence goes beyond the "military" influence exercised by either Wörner or Claes, partly because of the length of Allied Force's duration and the particular set of political circumstances during the bombing. On the sensitive issues of employing ground troops and selecting certain targets, Clark clearly listened to Solana's political advice on how to proceed militarily.

Solana (as well as Clark) has been criticized for seriously underestimating Milosevic's commitment to Kosovo, and for the faulty belief that Milosevic would succumb quickly to a minimal show of force by NATO.[58] It may be alleged that Solana and Clark were

---

58. William Arkin, "Operation Allied Force: 'The Most Precise Application of Air Power in History,'" in *War over Kosovo*, ed. Andrew J. Bacevich and Eliot A. Cohen (New York: Columbia University Press, 2001).

unable to effectively convey the extent of NATO's military threat to Milosevic, and that they failed in their goal of requiring his compliance with NATO's demands. Clearly, a misreading of the Serbs and Milosevic's commitment to maintaining political control of Kosovo was evident, but this criticism applies equally to all of NATO's capitals.[59] Solana cannot be faulted completely for this misjudgment, given the consensus for military action that all the allies had reached. Moreover, whether or not these criticisms are fair, they do not detract from Solana's diplomatic successes in promoting consensus within the alliance.

Just as Manfred Wörner and Willy Claes are only infrequently discussed as critical players in shaping NATO's transformation or Bosnia, references to Solana's place in NATO's evolution are similarly rare. Yet this chapter again demonstrates that NATO's post–Cold War secretary general played an instrumental role in influencing NATO's transition and, more specifically, on the use of force in Kosovo. Through a host of leadership decisions made in the NAC and through his relationship with the SACEUR, Solana personally contributed to Operation Allied Force in numerous ways. Solana's successor, Lord George Robertson, similarly proved instrumental in leading the alliance during the difficult decision to defend Turkey in 2003.

59. Ignatieff, *Virtual War*, 50–52.

5

George Robertson, Iraq, and the Defense of Turkey

Unlike the three previous secretaries general examined, Lord George Robertson, NATO's tenth secretary general, served in the changed atmosphere after the terrorist strikes on the United States on September 11, 2001. The attacks resulted in profoundly different foreign-policy outlooks from many countries. Most important among these changes, the United States soon asserted a willingness to use preemptive force to prevent future acts of terrorism. Such a doctrine is unilateral by definition, and it resulted in contentious policy differences between the United States and many of its allies at NATO.

In this chapter, the focus turns to Lord Robertson's management of the alliance when Turkey formally invoked Article 4 of the North Atlantic Treaty in February 2003. The invocation requested that NATO take defensive measures to protect Turkey from a potential military strike from Iraq. This issue, which Ambassador R. Nicholas Burns of the United States called "a crisis of credibility" for the alliance, was eventually resolved on February 16, 2003, when NATO, after considerable debate, approved the Article 4 request.[1] Like all the other post–Cold War secretaries general assessed thus far, Robertson was at the center of diplomatic action and played an instrumental role in managing the crisis.

1. Burns, quoted in Thomas Fuller, "Three Block NATO Aid for Turks on Iraq," *International Herald Tribune*, February 11, 2003, 1.

GEORGE ROBERTSON, 1999–2003

Lord George Robertson became NATO's tenth secretary general
on October 14, 1999. His selection as secretary general came without
the controversies that surrounded the appointments of Wörner,
Claes, and Solana. Lord Robertson's life in politics began in 1968,
when he became a union representative for the Scottish whiskey in-
dustry. In 1978, he was elected to serve in the United Kingdom
House of Commons as a member of the minority Labour Party.
Within the Labour Party, Robertson became the minority's chief
spokesperson on defense and foreign affairs. For nearly twenty
years, he remained in the House of Commons in the minority party,
until the 1997 elections, when Prime Minister Tony Blair and the
Labour Party gained majority status. At this time, Blair appointed
Robertson as the United Kingdom's defense secretary, and he
served in that office until his selection as NATO's secretary general

As U.K. defense secretary, Robertson was considered the most
forceful European advocate for NATO's bombing in Kosovo in
1999, a stance that made the Clinton administration look favorably
on him. During his tenure as defense secretary, he also ushered
through a politically successful defense transformation, which emphasized increasing the flexibility and mobility of the armed forces,
improving procurement standards, and heightening cooperation
among the U.K. armed services. Robertson's efforts were noteworthy, given that other defense-reform efforts had met stiff political
opposition in the United Kingdom. In successfully managing the
transition, Robertson consulted widely across the United Kingdom,
and his efforts eventually resulted in widespread consensus for the
changes implemented. During the process, the British public came
to appreciate his humility and self-effacing personality. In addition,
Robertson demonstrated great interest in advanced, technologically
sophisticated weaponry, which the European allies sorely lacked
during Operation Allied Force.[2]

Other candidates for NATO's top civilian position included,
again, the former Belgian prime minister, Jean-Luc Dehaene, and

2. Alexander Nicoll, "NATO Stage Would Be Ideal Platform for a Mod-
erniser," *Financial Times,* July 31, 1999, 10. For more on the limits of the European militaries during Allied Force, see John E. Peters, Stuart Johnson, Nora
Bensahel, Timothy Liston, and Traci Williams, *European Contributions to Operation Allied Force* (Washington, DC: RAND, 2001).

Denmark's defense minister, Hans Haekkerup. Dehaene had just been defeated in Belgium's June 1999 elections and was never considered a serious candidate by most of the allies. Haekkerup received objections from the French since Denmark was not a member of the West European Union. The only other serious candidate was Germany's defense minister, Rudolf Scharping, but he withdrew his name from consideration because of lackluster support and because he was still engaged in Germany's substantial defense reform. Robertson's name then surfaced, on July 31, 1999, when Prime Minister Blair announced his support for him, with the expressed backing of the United States, France, Italy, and Spain, which essentially sealed Robertson's selection as secretary general.[3] Thus, Lord Robertson entered NATO with high political credibility among all the major powers, and he had already earned transatlantic respect for his actions and policies across a host of defense-related issues.

In many respects, Robertson seemed to be the ideal candidate to lead NATO into a new era. He came to Brussels with the view that NATO should continue its evolution in meeting new security challenges. In the short term, Robertson was faced with a recently deployed, substantial NATO peacekeeping operation in Kosovo, which very quickly involved forty-six thousand soldiers, including two hundred Russians, whose government had opposed Operation Allied Force. In 2001, he was also confronted with additional instability in the Balkans, as Macedonian Albanians initiated military assaults on the Macedonian government, prompting NATO's Operation Essential Harvest, which helped produce a diplomatic solution between the warring factions.[4] Robertson has been viewed as a critical diplomat for the alliance during this time, who was personally helpful in negotiating an end to the violence.[5]

The terrorist attacks on September 11, 2001, which came only days after the crisis in Macedonia, however, ushered in a new era

3. Craig R. Whitney, "Britain Nominates Its Defense Secretary to Be Head of NATO," *New York Times*, July 31, 1999, A3.
4. On his initial views, see "Speech: Lord Robertson, NATO Secretary General to the Atlantic Treaty Association," October 10, 1999, NATO, http://www.nato.int/docu/speech/1999/s9910199.htm. On NATO's role in Macedonia, see "NATO's Role in the Former Yugoslav Republic of Macedonia," NATO, http://www.nato.int/fyrom/home.htm.
5. Joseph Ralston, former SACEUR, phone interview with author, August 9, 2004.

for the alliance. These events and the response at NATO are noteworthy for this analysis because they contributed to the systemic conditions that affected the Article 4 debate in 2003, and also because Robertson solidified his place in NATO's history through his actions at the time.

Soon after Al-Qaeda struck the United States, the American delegation at NATO called for a meeting of the North Atlantic Council to discuss the strikes.[6] After the meeting, the dean of the NATO ambassadors—the ambassador with the longest service at NATO—Canadian David Wright, suggested to Ambassador Burns that the political conditions were ripe for an invocation of Article 5, NATO's collective-defense agreement, which would be a first in NATO's history. The United States had not called for its application, but after some consideration and an early morning conversation with National Security Advisor Condoleezza Rice, at around 5 or 6 a.m. (EST) on September 12, Ambassador Burns conveyed to the NAC American approval for its invocation.[7]

Once the United States signaled its support, Robertson jumped at the opportunity to invoke Article 5. With the Bush administration immersed in the details of the terrorist strikes and the ongoing security of the United States, Robertson in many respects became the chief spokesperson for the decision. He viewed the conditions as a "use it or lose it" political scenario for the alliance and Article 5.[8] In the NAC discussions that followed, Robertson became the foremost advocate of Article 5. Where some tentative reservation and hesitation existed, Robertson personally phoned heads of state and foreign ministers, ensuring that their countries would allow Article 5 to go forward. Multiple interviewees indicate that Robertson placed

6. Much of the following information is based on interviews with NATO ambassadors and senior NATO staff officials in Brussels. While all senior staff members at NATO were interviewed on "background only," NATO ambassadors differed in how they were willing to be referenced. Those who were willing to be identified in general terms were Ambassadors R. Nicholas Burns of the United States, Dominique Struye de Swieland of Belgium, Jerzy M. Nowak of Poland, and Karel Kovanda of the Czech Republic. Two additional ambassadors were interviewed on background only.

7. R. Nicholas Burns, former U.S. ambassador to NATO, interview with author in Brussels, March 15, 2004.

8. Senior NATO official "A," interview with author in Brussels, March 15, 2004.

himself at the center of the discussions on Article 5 on behalf of the United States. Ambassador Burns has also noted that the secretary general "shepherded the Alliance's first-ever invocation of Article 5."[9] By the day's end, NAC approval was gained as the alliance stood willing to defend the United States. Given the historic nature of the decision, Robertson truly etched for himself a place in NATO's history on September 12, 2001.

The NAC decision was important symbolically in that it suggested transatlantic unity in support of the United States and the American military response that was sure to come in the future. For the first time in NATO's history, through Article 5's invocation, all allies stood side by side to jointly express their shared security interests. Even the French newspaper *Le Monde,* in the wake of the terrorist strikes, declared on September 12, "We are all Americans."[10]

Besides Robertson's role in the events resulting from the September 11 attack, during his tenure he became an aggressive advocate for improving member states' military capabilities. His position stemmed from his view that member states must be willing to transform themselves in order to play different and more diverse roles in international security, much as he had advocated as Britain's defense secretary. Throughout 2002, Robertson reminded the allies that modernization and defense transformation were needed by repeatedly emphasizing his mantra: "capabilities, capabilities, capabilities." At ministerial and summit meetings, Robertson would provide handouts to allied leaders with specific data showing how much (or how little) each member state spent on defense.[11] In one of his more blunt assessments of the European allies' military capabilities,

9. Quotation from "Remarks by Ambassador R. Nicholas Burns, U.S. Ambassador to NATO, Royal Institute for International Affairs, Chatham House, London," May 27, 2004, at http://nato.usmission.gov/ambassador/2004/20040527;London.htm; Ralston interview, August 9, 2004; senior NATO official "A" interview, March 15, 2004.

10. *Agence France Presse,* "'We are all Americans,' proclaims France's *Le Monde* Newspaper," September 12, 2001.

11. For examples of his mantra from his speeches, see "NATO after September 11," January 31, 2002, NATO, http://www.nato.int/docu/speech/2002/s020131a.htm; "NATO's Future," February 3, 2002, NATO, http://www.nato.int/docu/speech/2002/s020203a.htm; "Euro-Atlantic Security a Year after 11 September," September 12, 2002, NATO, http://www.nato.int/docu/speech/2002/s020912a.htm; "NATO: A Vision for 2012," October 3, 2002,

he noted, "The truth is that Europe remains a military pygmy." Such a statement was welcomed by the United States and was generally reflective of Robertson's sometimes direct diplomacy, but at the same time it was considered a poor choice of words and condescending by some of the European allies.[12]

His calls for improved military capabilities culminated at NATO's November 2002 Prague Summit, when the members agreed to the Prague Capabilities Initiative, which called for increased defense expenditures from all NATO members, as well as a NATO Response Force that would be capable of expeditious deployments to fight terrorism.[13] Although most of NATO's member states did not follow through on their political commitments for serious defense transformation and modernization, Robertson is still credited with playing a key role in helping the allies accept the initial Prague proposals, and with playing an instrumental role in moving the alliance to agree to these new commitments.[14] At Prague, NATO also invited seven Central and Eastern European states to join the alliance, including Bulgaria, Estonia, Latvia, Lithuania, Romania, Slovakia, and Slovenia. This expansion became official on March 29, 2004, and is the largest expansion in alliance history.

Robertson's role across all of these issues indicates that prior to the February 2003 invocation of Article 4, he had been an advocate for NATO's ongoing transformation and evolution, especially in light of the heightened challenge of terrorism. Much like Manfred Wörner, Robertson attempted to shape NATO's agenda through his

NATO, http://www.nato.int/docu/speech/2002/s021003a.htm; and "A Transformed NATO," October 22, 2002, NATO, http://www.nato.int/docu/speech/2002/s0210022a.htm; on the handouts, Ralston interview, August 9, 2004.

12. Quotation from Lord Robertson, "The Transatlantic Link," January 21, 2002, NATO, http://www.nato.int/docu/speech/2002/s020121a.htm; senior NATO official "B," interview with author in Brussels, March 15, 2004; senior NATO official "C," interview with author in Brussels, March 16, 2004; senior NATO official "A" interview, March 15, 2004; senior NATO official "D," interview with author in Brussels, March 16, 2004.

13. For a positive assessment of the Prague Summit achievements, see Michael Rühle, "NATO after Prague: Learning the Lessons of 9/11," *Parameters* 33, no. 2 (2003): 89–97. See also "Prague Summit Declaration," November 21, 2002, NATO, http://www.nato.int/docu/pr/2002/p02–127e.htm.

14. Burns interview, March 15, 2004; NATO ambassador "A," interview with author in Brussels, March 15, 2004.

own personal influence as secretary general, and in a number of instances was quite aggressive in lobbying for the policies he preferred. Whether it was alliance expansion, enhanced capabilities, or more generally a broader, global role for NATO, Robertson was an advocate of change. Like his predecessors, Robertson had demonstrated the secretary general's ability to influence transatlantic cooperation. His diplomatic skills were tested, however, when the alliance faced the crisis over Turkey's defense against Iraq in February 2003.

Systemic Conditions Facing Robertson

Before NATO's Article 4 crisis, two major systemic conditions existed that influenced the secretary general's ability to shape and influence policy. These structural factors were the United States' general distancing from NATO early in the Bush presidency and the profound policy differences between the Bush administration and most of the European allies over how to confront the ostensible security threat posed by Saddam Hussein. These transatlantic differences, which worked in tandem, were evident across a host of issues, and grew as the United States and Turkey eventually pushed NATO to approve of defensive measures prior to the war in Iraq.

Although Iraqi leader Saddam Hussein represented one of the most pressing security challenges for the United States since Hussein's invasion of Kuwait in 1990, NATO had always been, at best, a bystander on this issue. During Operation Desert Storm in 1991, NATO had no official military role, although analysts have suggested that NATO's previous defense planning was helpful to the United States as it led its coalition allies during the military operation. Upon Turkey's request, the alliance also took some defensive measures to protect Turkey against a potential attack from Iraq. These measures entailed the deployment of aircraft fighters from Belgium, Germany, and Italy to the Turkish-Iraqi border prior to Operation Desert Storm.[15] Yet, besides these steps, NATO stayed on

---

15. Marc Fisher, "NATO to Send Warplanes to Defend Turkey's Border with Iraq," *Washington Post,* January 3, 1991, A17. See NATO Press Release (91)2, "Statement by NATO Spokesperson," January 2, 1991, NATO, http://www.

the sidelines, remaining more focused on its own transformation under Manfred Wörner's leadership, which at the time centered on the historic changes to be implemented at the 1991 Rome Summit.

During the Clinton administration, NATO similarly remained out of the ongoing American-Iraqi conflict. In enforcing the no-fly zones over northern Iraq, the United States received some assistance from two NATO members: the United Kingdom and Turkey, given that the principal military base for staging these patrols was located at Incirlik, Turkey. In enforcing the southern no-fly zones, the United States received support from the United Kingdom and France, although French support ended after Operation Desert Fox in 1998, when American and British aircraft struck Iraq for four days after Iraq refused to comply with the United Nations Special Commission on Weapons Inspection.[16]

Similarly, on February 16, 2001, when newly inaugurated U.S. president George W. Bush and British prime minister Tony Blair jointly bombed Iraq for its ongoing violations of the no-fly zones, NATO was again not consulted and played no military role in these strikes. In short, the United States, with British support, defined the security agenda on how to address Iraq. Iraq security concerns were "out of area" for the alliance, were essentially controlled by the United States and Britain, and created no serious transatlantic diplomatic differences. Even though American military force had been used frequently in Iraq during the 1990s, it had not generated widespread European opposition, mostly because the military action was limited to air strikes and did not suggest the deployment of American ground forces to Iraq. The United States had passed the Iraqi Liberation Act in 1998, but this policy was aimed mostly at assisting Iraqi opposition groups, and did not entail overt American military action.

The diplomatic divide over Iraq between the Bush administration

---

nato.int/docu/pr/1991/p91–001e.htm. Turkey made this request, but did not invoke Article 4 of the North Atlantic Treaty in doing so. See also Stanley R. Sloan, *NATO, The European Union, and the Atlantic Community: The Transatlantic Bargain Reconsidered* (Lanham, MD: Rowman and Littlefield, 2003), 6.

16. "Operation Northern Watch," U.S. Defense Department, http://eucom.mil/Directorates/ECPA/Operations/onw/onw.htm; "Operation Southern Watch," U.S. Defense Department, http://www.milnet.com/pentagon/centcom/chap7/southw.htm.

and many of the European allies began early in the Bush presidency. Although a genuine interest for removing Hussein from power existed within the Bush administration almost immediately upon George W. Bush's inauguration, the issue of Iraq was placed aside temporarily after the September 11 strikes. Although Deputy Secretary of Defense Paul Wolfowitz and Secretary of Defense Donald Rumsfeld suggested in the aftermath of the terrorist strikes that the time was ripe for military action on Iraq, Bush allegedly removed Iraq from consideration on September 15, 2001, at the Camp David meetings when the principal American foreign-policy decision makers decided to concentrate on killing Osama Bin Laden and removing Afghanistan's ruling elite, the Taliban, from power.[17] On October 7, 2001, the United States initiated Operation Enduring Freedom and quickly eliminated the Taliban from its governing position. As already noted, transatlantic unity, arguably, was at its historical apex after September 11 with the invocation of Article 5.

Yet from a systemic/structural standpoint, the manner in which Enduring Freedom was conducted was relevant to the secretary general's leadership role. Although the invocation of Article 5 was approved, the Bush administration did not request NATO combat assistance in Enduring Freedom. And although fourteen NATO members eventually provided military assistance to the operation, as an institution NATO was not involved in the military operation or planning process. NATO did provide seven Airborne Warning and Control Systems (AWACS) for patrol of American airways to replace American AWACS operating in the war,[18] but otherwise the alliance's essential absence from Enduring Freedom had a systemic result that later affected the debate over Turkey's defense. NATO's absence created the feeling among some Europeans that the United States had disregarded NATO.

Given the Europeans' deficient military capabilities and the additional time and security risk associated with multilateral planning,

17. Bob Woodward, *Bush at War* (New York: Simon and Schuster, 2002), 83–85. See also Ron Suskind, *The Price of Loyalty: George W. Bush, the White House, and the Education of Paul O'Neill* (New York: Simon and Schuster, 2004), 96–97, for the Bush administration's early interest in using force in Iraq.

18. Lord George Robertson, "Speech by the Secretary General at the Annual Conference of the Defence and Society," January 31, 2002, NATO, http://www.nato.int/docu/speech/2002/s020121a.htm.

the United States may have chosen wisely to proceed without NATO. The alliance's "war by committee" in Operation Allied Force, while victorious, left a deep wound in transatlantic military relations, as the European militaries proved to be deficient in weaponry, communications equipment, and aircraft capabilities, among other areas. The joint military planning that took place in 1999, especially the intra-alliance debates over targeting choices, were deeply dissatisfying to many. Certainly, a case can be made that NATO's victory in Kosovo had a myopic quality: although Milosevic was defeated through multilateral military strikes, profound dissatisfaction remained with NATO planning procedures and its ability to wage war.[19]

At the same time, others maintain that the American decision to neglect NATO was a serious diplomatic mistake that widened the political divide between the Bush administration and Europe, a relationship that was damaged already by the Bush administration's disregard for the Kyoto Protocol, its favorable views on the United States' National Missile Defense, and its opposition to the United Nations' International Criminal Court.[20] Clearly, the systemic consequence of the unilateral nature of Enduring Freedom played some role in heightening an already growing divide between the United States and many of the European allies.

In a move that further increased the growing transatlantic differences, the Bush administration in August 2002 aggressively and openly elevated the issue of Iraq onto its national security agenda. Iraq took on fundamentally new political and strategic dimensions as the Bush administration first argued publicly, through Vice President Richard Cheney, that Saddam Hussein had weapons of mass destruction and posed a direct threat to the world.[21] Such state-

19. David S. Yost, "The NATO Capabilities Gap and the European Union," *Survival* 42, no. 4 (2000–2001): 97–128; John E. Peters et al., *European Contributions to Operation Allied Force*, 53–69; Sean Kay, "What Went Wrong with NATO," *Cambridge Review of International Affairs* 18, no. 1 (2005): 76.

20. See Strobe Talbott, "From Prague to Baghdad: NATO at Risk," *Foreign Affairs* 81, no. 6 (2002): 46–58; and Roger Cohen, "America the Roughneck (Through Europe's Eyes)," *New York Times*, May 6, 2002, A10.

21. Richard Cheney, "Vice President Speaks at VFW 103rd National Convention," White House Office of the Press Secretary, August 26, 2002, http://www.whitehouse.gov/news/releases/2002/08/print/20020826.html.

ments generated some domestic criticism and considerable international opposition. In the United States, members of Congress demanded that President Bush gain congressional approval before going to war in Iraq.[22] Abroad, most states in the world declared that the Bush administration's suggestions regarding preemptive military action were illegal, arguing that UN Security Council approval was needed before force could be used. In response, the Bush administration turned to the United Nations. In the president's annual address to the UN General Assembly, Bush called upon the organization to address the threat that Hussein posed, while simultaneously suggesting that the United Nations was acting akin to the League of Nations prior to the Second World War, when it failed to face Adolf Hitler.[23]

After the Bush administration agreed to attempt a diplomatic solution on Iraq through the United Nations, which resulted eventually in UN Security Council Resolution 1441 and a weapons-inspection process, transatlantic differences reached their nadir when the Bush administration maintained that Iraq was hiding weapons of mass destruction and was not cooperating with the UN inspectors. In contrast, most European countries, led by France and Germany, argued for the continuation of diplomacy and the UN inspection process. Although gaining the UN Security Council endorsement was clearly a diplomatic victory for the Bush administration, the diplomatic "consensus" achieved at the United Nations had a short life span, as transatlantic differences quickly resumed.[24]

The Prague Summit in November 2002 resulted in important

22. John Kerry, "We Still Have a Choice on Iraq," *New York Times*, September 6, 2002, A23. Once the war powers question reached the House and Senate floors, however, the debate over the president's "authority" to use force was limited. See Ryan C. Hendrickson, "Clinton, Bush, Congress and War Powers: A Comparative Analysis of the Military Strikes on Iraq and Bin Laden" (paper presented at the Woodrow Wilson Institute, May 17, 2004), at http://wwics.si.edu/events/docs/hendrickson.pdf.

23. George W. Bush, "Address to the United Nations General Assembly in New York City," *Weekly Compilation of Presidential Documents* 38 (September 16, 2002): 1529–34; Steven Erlanger, "Traces of Terror: Perspectives; German Leader's Warning: War Plan Is a Huge Mistake," *New York Times*, September 5, 2002, A1.

24. John Tagliabue, "Threats and Responses: Brussels; European Nations Fall Short of Consensus on Iraq Report," *New York Times*, January 28, 2003, A12.

achievements for NATO, including alliance membership expansion, a promise by all members to enhance their military capabilities, and plans for a NATO Response Force, but Iraq remained an issue. Although at Prague the allies called upon Hussein to disarm and cooperate with the United Nations, strong differences over Iraq still dominated the political and diplomatic agenda.[25]

As American-European differences grew, Secretary of Defense Donald Rumsfeld created additional tensions when he suggested on January 22, 2003, the presence of a "new" and an "old" Europe, and said that "the center of gravity [within NATO Europe] is shifting to the east and there are a lot of new members."[26] The implication was that the "new" Europe, including such states as Bulgaria, Poland, Romania, and the Baltic countries, was forward-looking and progressive in meeting new security challenges, while the "old" Europe of Germany and France was divorced from the realities of modern global security. Rumsfeld's statement generated a considerable backlash from France and Germany, and it had parallels with an earlier statement he had made, in June 2002, when he maintained that "effective multilateralism" may require "coalitions of the willing," which also suggested a distancing from the United States' traditional NATO allies.[27] Thus, the differences between the United States and its key NATO allies were especially pronounced in the days immediately before the Article 4 issue was raised. Transatlantic differences, which were evident on many fronts, generally shaped the structural environment prior to and in the initial stages of the debate over defending Turkey.

On December 4, 2002, the U.S. deputy secretary of defense, Paul Wolfowitz, visited NATO headquarters in Brussels. At a meeting of the North Atlantic Council, Wolfowitz presented a list of military options and proposals related to Iraq for the alliance to consider. These proposals, which were framed in the context of a potential

25. Patrick E. Tyler, "Threats and Responses: The Alliance; NATO Leaders Say Iraq Must Disarm," *New York Times*, November 22, 2002, A1.

26. Rumsfeld, quoted in Geir Moulson, "Rumsfeld's 'Old Europe' Comment Provokes Angry Rebuttals in France and Germany," *Associated Press*, January 23, 2003.

27. United States Department of Defense Press Release, "Secretary Rumsfeld Remarks as Delivered at the Marshall Center's Tenth Anniversary," June 12, 2003, at http://defenselink.mil/releases/2003/nr20030612-0095.html.

war with Iraq and were to be considered only as consultations with the NATO allies, included NATO military assistance to Turkey, including AWACS and Patriot missiles. Wolfowitz also noted that NATO could potentially aid Iraqi citizens through humanitarian assistance and could provide access to airspace or airfields to NATO members in the event of an Iraqi war. Another policy idea included logistical assistance to those allies who would participate in combat operations in Iraq. In addition, Wolfowitz suggested that NATO troops could replace American forces on NATO bases in Europe, since additional U.S. troops might be needed in a war in Iraq.[28]

While some at NATO applauded the United States' interest in consulting with the allies, these proposals were not formal requests but rather only ideas to consider at the time. Moreover, Wolfowitz's proposals were not followed by an intensive lobbying effort by the United States in Brussels. The Iraq/Turkey question was not considered again until mid-January 2003, when the American delegation brought the issue to the NAC for more formal discussions of how the alliance could work multilaterally to assist Turkey in the event of war. Although it was clear that the United States had in some manner attempted to insert NATO into the diplomatic/military dialogue on Iraq, at the same time some European leaders viewed Wolfowitz's proposals as an American "rediscovery" of NATO.[29]

In light of these systemic conditions, Lord Robertson acted initially with considerable caution on the issue of Iraq. In the latter

28. United States Department of Defense News Transcript, "Media Stakeout at NATO with Deputy Secretary Wolfowitz," December 4, 2002, at http://defenselink.mil/transcripts/2002/t12052002 1204stakeout.html; Jerzy M. Nowak, "Changes in NATO and Poland's National Interest," in *International Security in a Time of Change: Threats, Concepts, Institutions*, ed. Hans J. Giessman, Roman Kuzniar, and Zdzislaw Lachowski (Baden-Baden: Nomos Verlagsgesellschaft, 2004), 335–36; Michael R. Gordon, "Threats and Responses: The Allies; U.S. Asks NATO Nations to Offer Forces for an Iraq Campaign," *New York Times*, December 5, 2002, A27; Vernon Loeb and Thomas E. Ricks, "Aid from NATO Allies Asked for Iraqi War; Troops, Noncombat Support Sought," *Washington Post*, December 6, 2002, A35.

29. NATO ambassador "A" interview, March 15, 2004, and phone interview with author, August 26, 2004. On the absence of American lobbying efforts, see Michael R. Gordon, "U.S. Asks NATO for Aid in Building Combat Power in the Gulf," *International Herald Tribune*, January 18, 2003, 10.

months of 2002, when Iraq had moved to the center of the international stage, Robertson refrained from introducing Iraq specifically in his public speeches. Rather, most of his speeches focused on NATO's relevance after September 11, as well as his goals for the Prague Summit in November. In this regard, he clearly avoided the transatlantic debate over Iraq. Robertson's strategy contrasts quite strongly with Manfred Wörner's aggressive calls for NATO engagement in the Balkans when the transatlantic political divide was similarly deep. Wörner challenged member states to unite on the difficult issue of Bosnia. Although Javier Solana refrained from public appeals for a NATO policy change toward the Balkans in 1998, he lobbied quietly for NATO engagement within NATO corridors. Robertson generally chose to keep quiet on Iraq among the ambassadors.

Given that the United States showed limited interest in formally placing Iraq on NATO's agenda, even after Wolfowitz's visit to Brussels in December 2002, Robertson clearly decided to limit public diplomacy on questions regarding Iraq.[30] Even if Robertson had asserted a leadership role, he likely would have faced intense opposition from many allies. In recognizing his political limitations, much like Willy Claes, Robertson chose to wait for some systemic shift before attempting to lead the alliance in a new direction. Like that of most secretaries general, Robertson's leadership on Iraq came to fruition primarily within the NAC and in the private diplomacy that eventually resolved the Article 4 invocation.

Organizational Leadership

Many of those who served with Lord Robertson considered him to be a forceful and independent chairman of the NAC. Perhaps most like Manfred Wörner, Robertson would willingly insert his personal views into NAC debates and then defend them vigorously. His deep knowledge of defense and military issues was also an aspect of his leadership that worked to his benefit. With this background, stemming from his previous leadership of the United Kingdom's Defense Ministry, Robertson could not be "out-wonked" on defense-policy matters.[31]

30. Gordon, "U.S. Asks NATO for Aid," 10.
31. Burns interview, March 15, 2004.

Many of Robertson's colleagues at NATO also note his gift of humor and his self-deprecating jokes, which he would insert effectively into particularly tense moments within the NAC. His ability to use humor and wit with consistent effectiveness makes Robertson stand apart from all other secretaries general in the post–Cold War era, and compares only with Joseph Luns during the Cold War. As a diplomatic tool, Robertson's jokes were noted frequently among his colleagues and were a unique facet of his leadership style.[32]

One serious limitation on Robertson's NAC leadership, however, was his inability to speak French. Robertson had attempted to learn French, but his efforts had yielded few results, which he openly joked about on numerous occasions. Although Robertson made notable self-deprecating remarks regarding his Francophone deficiencies, such jokes were not always considered humorous by some members of the alliance. When his Francophone limitations were coupled with the profound policy differences that surfaced between France, Belgium, and the United States, the result was a genuine political hurdle that cannot be neglected. While English and French are the two official languages of the alliance, during moments of crisis, especially, the French and the Belgians prefer to speak in their native language. Robertson's inability to speak French may also have contributed to what many at NATO viewed as a personality clash between Robertson and French ambassador to NATO Benoit D'Aboville. Although some at NATO maintain that D'Aboville had a confrontational personality, Robertson's inability to speak French seemed only to exacerbate the already difficult political climate at NATO during the Article 4 crisis.[33]

More specific to the alliance's debate over whether to provide military defenses to Turkey, much evidence places Robertson at the center of diplomatic action in January and February 2003. The NAC

---

32. Ibid.; NATO ambassador "A" interview, March 15, 2004; NATO ambassador "B," interview with author in Brussels, March 15, 2004; NATO ambassador "C," interview with author in Brussels, March 15, 2004; Jerzy M. Nowak, Polish ambassador to NATO, interview with author in Brussels, March 17, 2004.

33. Nowak interview, March 17, 2004; senior NATO official "A" interview, March 15, 2004; NATO ambassador "D," interview with author in Brussels, March 16, 2004; senior NATO official "C" interview, March 16, 2004. See also Judy Dempsey, "The First Lord of NATO Trips on the Lines of Command," *Financial Times*, February 15, 2003, 13.

began to formally discuss the alliance's role in the issue on January 17, 2003, when the United States urged the council to discuss how best to defend Turkey in case of a war in Iraq. Based upon Wolfowitz's earlier proposals, the list consisted of several military options, including using AWACS, deploying Patriot missiles, using NATO naval forces to guard the Mediterranean, using NATO bases as potential launching pads for strikes on Iraq, and increasing European forces at NATO bases and NATO peacekeeping operations in the Balkans to replace American troops who might be needed in Iraq.[34]

Upon the United States' official request, and with the issue now formally on the agenda for discussion, Robertson became an active supporter of the American position. While the secretary general could not necessarily prevent the United States from placing the issue on NATO's agenda, he could have discouraged it through either public or private diplomacy. Instead, Robertson quite quickly sided with the American position.[35] Moreover, after approximately a week and a half of ongoing NAC deliberation, Robertson noted publicly that the American-proposed military steps were "prudent" steps for the alliance to consider. In tune with the Bush administration's views on the United Nations weapons inspectors at the time, Robertson added, "It is not an issue of what the inspectors might or might not find. The resolution is very explicit that he is the one who has to prove, by the use of clear and convincing audit that he has got rid of those weapons of mass destruction."[36] In this regard, Robertson played an important role in helping the United States set the agenda for the alliance, and almost exactly echoed the American position. Unlike the French and the Germans, who placed more of their policy emphasis on what the weapons inspectors were able to find, Robertson emphasized Saddam Hussein's degree of cooperation with the inspectors. Thus, once the Bush administration decided to work through NATO, Robertson quickly chose sides and became a vocal advocate for the American position.

34. Bradley Graham, "U.S. Official Appeals to NATO for Military Support," *Washington Post,* January 17, 2003, A15; Gordon, "U.S. Asks NATO for Aid," 10.

35. NATO ambassador "E," interview with author in Brussels, March 16, 2004; senior NATO official "A," phone interview with author, October 20, 2004.

36. "Questions and Answers with NATO Secretary General, Lord Robertson," January 27, 2003, NATO, http://www.nato.int.docu/speech/2003/s030127a.htm.

As discussions ensued over the request, and as alliance negotiations became stalled over the appropriateness of NATO's defense of Turkey because some members of the alliance saw such a move as premature and too sympathetic to the Bush administration's approach toward Iraq, Robertson again demonstrated the potential leadership role that a secretary general can exercise through his invocation of the silence procedure, just as Javier Solana had done when he sought to grant SACEUR General Wesley Clark the necessary political approval for hitting Option III military targets.[37] As discussed in Chapter 4, the silence procedure is one tactic that can be useful in promoting consensus. As long as silence is not broken before a stated time set by the secretary general, the secretary general's policy proposal stands and consensus is then reached. The silence procedure can also be useful in that it allows the alliance to move forward with a decision when a state may still disagree with the policy direction. In other words, a state may not completely agree with NATO, but it also may not wish to obstruct NATO's ability to act on the given issue. Thus, the procedure, if used in the appropriate political circumstances, can be an effective diplomatic tool in promoting consensus.[38]

Robertson's decision to apply the silence procedure quickly presented the alliance with a major and openly visible crisis, as Belgium, France, and Germany almost immediately broke silence publicly.[39] Since the same three states had expressed such open and vocal opposition to the direction of American foreign policy toward Iraq at the United Nations, Robertson's tactical decision involved great political risk for himself and the alliance. Given the almost immediate decision to break the silence in a public manner, and now

37. Lord George Robertson, "Statement," February 6, 2003, NATO, http://www.nato.int/docu/speech/2003/s030206a.htm.

38. Robertson had previously used the silence procedure effectively. See Constant Brand, "NATO Members Approve U.S. Request for Military Assistance in Anti-terrorism Campaign," *Associated Press*, October 4, 2001; *Agence France Presse*, "NATO Launches Macedonia Operation to Collect Rebel Weapons," August 22, 2001; and *Czech News Agency*, "Govt to Name NATO Summit Commissioner, Vondra Often Mentioned," March 24, 2001.

39. Craig S. Smith and Richard Bernstein, "Threats and Responses: Diplomacy; Three Members of NATO and Russia Resist U.S. on Iraq Plans," *New York Times*, February 11, 2003, A1.

with an open feud at NATO, Robertson's decision proved to be a diplomatic gamble that arguably heightened tensions within the alliance and made the allies' political differences a news item across the world.

When silence was broken, Turkey followed by taking the unprecedented step of formally invoking NATO's Article 4 for the first time in the alliance's history. Article 4 reads, "The Parties will consult together whenever, in the opinion of any of them, the territorial integrity, political independence or security of any of the Parties is threatened."[40] Robertson, U.S. ambassador to NATO Nicholas Burns, and Turkish ambassador to NATO Ahmet Üzümcü had all been in discussion during Robertson's silence procedure, so Robertson understood that Turkey would invoke Article 4 in the event that silence was broken.[41]

When Article 4 was invoked, and as the alliance continued to struggle over whether to accept Turkey's defensive request, Robertson's organizational leadership role in promoting consensus may have been hurt by lackluster diplomatic support from Ambassador Üzümcü, who presented the Article 4 request. During much of the crisis, Üzümcü said little during the debates and seemed at times to be ambivalent regarding what NATO could provide to Turkey.[42] His actions were likely connected to the political uncertainty in Turkey after the November 2002 election, in which Recep Tayyip Erdogan's Muslim-based Justice and Development party won and later was unwilling to support the United States' request to place American ground forces in Turkey prior to Operation Iraqi Freedom.[43]

With the silence broken and the open political divide at NATO visible to all, Robertson allowed the debate to go on for four more days, until he personally made the decision to utilize NATO's Defense Planning Committee (DPC), from which France had withdrawn in 1966. With this decision, Robertson clearly exercised some independence as secretary general. It was his decision to utilize the

40. North Atlantic Treaty, Article 4. See Appendix.
41. Burns interview, March 15, 2004.
42. Senior NATO official "B" interview, March 15, 2004; senior NATO official "C" interview, March 16, 2004; senior NATO official "D" interview, March 16, 2004.
43. Michael R. Gordon, "Threats and Responses: Turkey," *New York Times*, December 9, 2002, A1.

DPC, which nearly ensured that the Article 4 request would be approved since it removed France from the decision-making process. Robertson also exercised some independence by choosing to wait as long as he did to go to the DPC.[44]

Another critical element of the debate, to the surprise of nearly all at NATO, came after Robertson's decision to utilize the DPC had been made as Belgium still vigorously opposed the Article 4 application. When Robertson moved the question to the DPC, it was anticipated that the Belgians would simply fall in line behind the Germans, who had signaled their willingness to approve of Article 4 once in the DPC.[45] Yet Belgium made very high political demands on the rest of the allies and most importantly the United States regarding the actual language to be used in the Article 4 approval. In the final hours of the negotiations on February 16, 2003, Ambassador Dominique Struye de Swieland of Belgium was accompanied in these sessions by his foreign minister and a representative from Belgian prime minister Guy Verhofstadt's office. In attempting to resolve the crisis, Robertson was again at the center of the negotiations between the United States and Belgium. With consensus still not reached, Robertson placed intense pressure on the Belgians to join with the rest of the alliance. During the discussions, Robertson personally telephoned Verhofstadt to lobby for his country's support for Article 4's approval. In his conversations, Robertson relentlessly advocated two positions: First, he pointed out that the Article 4 request was purely a military decision that had only defensive implications for the alliance. In making this case, he tried forcefully to separate the Article 4 issue from American foreign policy toward Iraq. Second, as both Wörner and Solana had done during times of crisis, Robertson appealed to the need for alliance solidarity, arguing that Belgian opposition to Article 4 would have a long-term harmful impact on NATO's credibility.[46]

44. NATO ambassador "B" felt that the United States would have preferred a more expeditious move to the DPC (interview, March 15, 2004). Robertson took personal responsibility for invoking the DPC. See Lord George Robertson, "Building a Transatlantic Consensus," February 20, 2003, NATO, http://www.nato.int/docu/speech/2003/s030220b.htm.

45. NATO ambassador "A" interview, March 15, 2004.

46. Nowak interview, March 17, 2004; NATO ambassador "C" interview, March 15, 2004; Keith B. Richburg, "NATO Agrees to Begin Aid to Turkey," *Washington Post*, February 17, 2003, A1.

In these discussions with Belgium and the United States, Robertson was personally involved in drafting the decision sheet with his
British assistant, John Day. In attempting to resolve the crisis, Robertson met with the United States and Belgium together and separately to find the necessary compromise language.[47] By the day's
end, Belgian demands were met with inclusion of a reference to the
United Nations in the actual decision sheet, which read: "In this
context, the DPC . . . recalls the provisions of Article 1 of the North
Atlantic Treaty, and in particular the undertaking of Allies to refrain
in their international relations from the threat of use of force in any
manner inconsistent with the purposes of the United Nations." The
United Nations reference, coupled with what was perceived as limited defensive measures to be taken by NATO, enabled the final approval for Article 4.[48]

Robertson played a critical leadership role in reaching the Article 4
decision, but its ultimate military value was questionable. A case
can be made that the final resolution had (at best) a myopic quality,
was little more than a symbolic statement by NATO, and did severe
political damage to transatlantic relations. Germany had already offered to provide bilateral defensive assistance to Turkey by loaning
Patriot missiles and AWACS to the Netherlands, who could then assist Turkey. Thus, the approval of Article 4 did little more than what
Germany had already offered, and was a relatively small defensive
step.[49] Moreover, the final decision came after a public "breaking
of silence," through the open invocation of Article 4, and through
the use of the DPC—all of which occurred as the world watched
the allies struggle to find consensus. It was felt by some ambassadors and NATO staff members that Robertson pushed too aggressively and quickly for a resolution before consensus had been
reached, and that he chose to side with the American position too
quickly. It has also been suggested that Robertson's own overconfi-

47. NATO ambassador "A" interview, March 15, 2004, and phone interview,
August 26, 2004.

48. Quotation from NATO Press Release, "Decision Sheet of the Defence
Planning Committee," February 16, 2003, NATO, http://www.nato.int/docu/
pr/2003/p030216e.htm; NATO ambassador "A" interview, March 15, 2004.

49. NATO ambassador "A" interview, March 15, 2004; Richard Bernstein and
Steven R. Weisman, "Threats and Responses: Alliance; NATO Settles Rift over
Aid to Turks in Case of a War," *New York Times*, February 17, 2003, A1.

dence and perceived diplomatic strengths may have been a factor exacerbating the crisis.[50]

At the same time, the United States, NATO's most powerful member, had clearly chosen to seek NATO support on this issue. Had Robertson not sided with the United States, it potentially would have been a devastating political blow to his own personal relationship with the United States and, by extension, the United States' future interest in working with NATO. As the previous chapters have demonstrated, the secretary general relies heavily upon American support to promote consensus during difficult times. The secretary general's ability to lead is often tied to American backing. Thus, Robertson was placed in an unusually difficult political position. The signs were clear from the onset of the debate that France, Germany, Belgium, and even Luxembourg were willing to debate and perhaps outright oppose any NATO endorsement regarding any issue related to Iraq.[51] Yet a refusal to wholeheartedly back the American policy request, especially when the request had support from a number of the NATO allies (including the British), would have simultaneously done serious political damage to his own position as secretary general.

Whether the crisis was a result of the United States' misreading of the diplomatic mood among the allies, Turkey's ambivalent diplomatic tactics within the NAC, or Robertson's own overconfidence and specific leadership decisions (or a mixture of all of these factors) is impossible to determine conclusively. Whatever the reason(s) for the crisis, Robertson's leadership role in the NAC was instrumental in shaping NATO's agenda throughout the crisis and, in the end, was a critical factor in reaching consensus after this especially difficult period in NATO's history.

Working with the SACEUR: Robertson and Joseph Ralston

Comparatively, Robertson's leadership in the Article 4 crisis represents a slightly different case study from those in the three pre-

50. Senior NATO official "A" interview, March 15, 2004; senior NATO official "E," interview with author in Brussels, March 16, 2004.
51. Keith B. Richburg, "NATO Blocked on Iraq Decision; France, Germany Lead Opposition to War," *Washington Post*, January 23, 2003, A1.

ceding chapters. In this case, NATO did not engage in military combat, although it did approve of defensive measures to protect Turkey.
In all the other cases examined, NATO used force. Moreover, just as
the official American request to NATO over Turkey was initiated,
the supreme allied commander, Europe, General Joseph Ralston, re-
tired from his position at NATO and was replaced on January 17,
2003, with General James Jones. In addition, after Jones replaced
Ralston, Jones did not play a central diplomatic or negotiating role
on Article 4. Robertson led the diplomatic efforts among the allies.
Thus, in a number of ways the SACEUR–secretary general relationship here is much different from those of the previous secretaries
general examined. Yet much insight can still be gained by studying
Robertson's relationship with the SACEUR. Since General Ralston
served as SACEUR for the longest period of time with Robertson,
and since Ralston was still SACEUR in the weeks leading up to the
Article 4 crisis, the focus here is on Robertson's relationship with
Ralston.

On Robertson's general professional relationship with the SACEUR,
much evidence suggests that Ralston and Robertson worked together quite closely. In the first real political crisis that they faced
together, Ralston was especially impressed with Robertson's diplomatic skills and his ability to promote peace in Macedonia when
political violence erupted in the summer of 2001. In terms of communication, on average they spoke about every other day. Moreover, on Tuesday mornings during Ralston's tenure they would
hold a joint video conference between themselves and key military
and political subordinates, as Ralston was located at NATO military
headquarters in Mons, Belgium, and Robertson was in Brussels.
Such extensive communication also included telephone calls; when
necessary, Ralston would call Robertson at his private residence in
Scotland.[52]

Their close communication also extended to NAC meetings. Although Ralston never sought Robertson's approval or formal support prior to a NAC presentation, Ralston maintains that the secretary
general was never uninformed about or surprised by what he said

52. Ralston interview, August 9, 2004. This close communication between the
SACEUR and Robertson was also supported by senior NATO official "B,"
phone interview with author, October 27, 2004.

or presented to the NATO ambassadors. Ralston's views are supported by those who witnessed their interactions in the NAC. In these sessions, the SACEUR and the secretary general had the same policy preferences and ideological beliefs and did not find themselves at odds.[53] In general, much like Javier Solana and Wesley Clark's working relationship, the relationship between Robertson and Ralston suggests one of mutual respect and frequent communication.

Although Robertson had extensive knowledge of defense issues and weapons systems, he granted the SACEUR wide discretion on military questions for the alliance. In reality it can be difficult to separate NATO's "military" questions from its "political" questions, which fall more clearly under the secretary general's sphere of policy influence. Yet, like Willy Claes working with George Joulwan, Robertson did not clash with Ralston over military-logistical matters, as Robertson allowed for the SACEUR's military judgment and discretion.[54]

On the issue of Iraq and Turkey, despite NATO's diplomatic absence on the issue in 2002, Ralston and Robertson communicated closely throughout the fall of 2002 as the United States moved closer toward war. With the United States applying increased diplomatic pressure on Iraq, Robertson requested that Ralston keep him informed of all critical developments in American foreign policy. Likewise, as the United States attempted to gain Turkish support for a deployment of U.S. ground forces to Turkey, Ralston privately kept Robertson informed of key American diplomatic and military developments. Much of Ralston's work at the time centered around his role as commander of the U.S. European Command, not as SACEUR. Ralston, however, still maintained private consultations with the secretary general. It is Ralston's view that Robertson wanted NATO to be engaged in some capacity if there was going to be a war with Iraq.[55] Thus, at the personal level Robertson and Ralston maintained close ties as the American build-up proceeded, despite NATO's absence from the diplomacy on the issue of Iraq.

53. Ralston interview, August 9, 2004; senior NATO official "B" interview, October 27, 2004; senior NATO official "A" interview, October 20, 2004.
54. Ralston interview, August 9, 2004.
55. Ibid.

Conclusion

Much like the previous cases examined in this book, this case study of NATO's decision to provide defensive measures to Turkey and of George Robertson's role in fostering transatlantic consensus for this action again demonstrates the critical role and potential influence of NATO's secretary general. Robertson's actions and decisions had significant impact on the alliance's ability to reach consensus, and similarly had a broader impact on the alliance that went beyond the invocation of Article 4.

At the systemic level, Robertson faced profound challenges. With transatlantic differences so deep over Iraq, Robertson chose to focus his political energy on the Prague Summit, and made no public attempts to engage NATO in the political and diplomatic discourse surrounding Iraq. Iraq largely stayed off Robertson's agenda as secretary general. In many respects, Robertson acted as Willy Claes did during the Bosnia crisis, when Claes waited for the United States to openly turn to NATO before he began to aggressively push the allies in a new policy direction. In contrast, Robertson's leadership was different from that of Manfred Wörner, who advocated for NATO engagement in the Balkans long before alliance consensus was reached. For Robertson, the systemic challenges were too great to overcome, and until a specific request came from the United States in January 2003, Robertson did not insert himself publicly into the international diplomatic debate over Iraq.

Within the NAC, however, Robertson was at the center of nearly every key decision made during the Article 4 crisis. Once the United States brought the issue forward, Robertson supported the principle of discussing the issue and teamed with the United States immediately as an advocate for the policy. It was his decision to employ the silence procedure, it was his decision to activate the DPC, and he was the central mediator between the United States and Belgium in the last hours of the crisis, when Belgium surprised all with its eleventh-hour objections. Robertson's efforts and his tenacious diplomacy resulted in a successful resolution of the crisis. At the same time, he was a central player as the crisis heightened, which many analysts, NATO staffers, and some delegations at NATO viewed as the alliance's worst hour in recent memory. In many respects, this case illustrates the difficult balancing act that a secretary genera can face, and the systemic difficulties caused when American foreign policy has distanced itself from its European allies.

On Robertson's relationship with the SACEUR, most evidence suggests that he and General Ralston maintained close contact in the weeks prior to the Article 4 crisis. Like the Solana-Clark relationship, Robertson and Ralston generally shared the same philosophical outlook for the alliance and maintained their cooperative approach during NAC sessions. Given that this particular case study did not include combat, and that the alliance was undergoing a change in SACEURs when this crisis occurred, fewer leadership insights are gained at this level on Robertson—with the important exception that while the United States was pursuing Iraq without NATO support, Ralston and Robertson still maintained close private consultations.

In sum, Robertson's role in the Article 4 crisis again demonstrates the critical role a secretary general plays in guiding and fostering consensus at NATO. Once the issue was brought to the NAC, Robertson was at the center of NATO's diplomacy. An examination of this decision absent some recognition of Robertson's role misses a critical component of NATO's decision-making process and the manner in which NATO evolves. More broadly, Robertson, at minimum, was a central player in one of NATO's most openly divisive debates, which highlighted the profound differences at NATO over Iraq and led many to question NATO's future relevance in transatlantic security. In many respects, NATO is still struggling to overcome the transatlantic divide that became so pronounced in February 2003.

6
NATO's Post–Cold War Secretary General

Considerable research has been devoted to NATO's post–Cold War transformation, including examinations of its uses of force, its historic decisions to expand its membership, its cooperative military training programs with the former communist states of Central and Eastern Europe, and the strategic-doctrinal changes it approved for its new security milieu. What is clear, despite what some scholars predicted in the aftermath of the Soviet Union's collapse, is that NATO transformed itself into an effective and relevant military alliance during the 1990s.[1] By some measurements the alliance superceded the United Nations as the world's most prominent international organization, as NATO eventually authorized and employed successful military operations to address the humanitarian crises taking place in the Balkans; no other multilateral institution could find the political will or necessary resources to meet the security challenge.

Although many factors contributed to NATO's transformation, including the Clinton administration's willingness to reform NATO, as well as the Europeans' ongoing support for the alliance, the preceding chapters demonstrate that the secretaries general often played

1. The foremost skeptics on NATO were John J. Mearsheimer, "Back to the Future: Instability in Europe after the Cold War," *International Security* 15, no. 1 (1990): 5–57; Kenneth N. Waltz, "The Emerging Structure of International Politics," *International Security* 18, no. 2 (1993): 44–79; and Christopher Layne, "Superpower Disengagement," *Foreign Policy* 77 (Winter 1989–1990): 17–40.

nstrumental roles in shaping alliance policies on use-of-force issues. These findings contrast with the previous literature on NATO's secretaries general during the Cold War; these men are viewed as talented and skilled diplomats, but are still depicted as more distant players in the broader arena of transatlantic diplomacy.[2] Owing to new leadership opportunities at NATO and the alliance's broader mission in the Soviet Union's absence, the post–Cold War secretaries general played critical roles at NATO when military action was adopted and implemented, and thus were key contributors in shaping the alliance's post–Cold War evolution. Whether it was Manfred Wörner, Willy Claes, Javier Solana, or George Robertson, NATO's secretaries general utilized an assortment of diplomatic tactics and alliance tools to individually make an impact on major political and military decisions at NATO. Their influence, however, varies according to the leadership forum examined.

Leadership at the Systemic Level

At the systemic level, the preceding chapters demonstrate the often profound political limitations that exist on the ability of any secretary general to lead the alliance. NATO's member states, especially the United States, still largely define the parameters for NATO's engagement in international security affairs. Without a semblance of consensus, especially when the United States refrains from steering the alliance toward a specific policy objective, the secretary general can often do little to change the systemic conditions. In recognizing these limitations, Willy Claes and George Robertson both were cautious in calling for NATO engagement in Bosnia and with regard to Iraq until American foreign-policy makers shifted in a new direction or specified their request. Javier Solana lobbied only quietly for systemic policy changes at NATO headquarters during the early stages of the Kosovo crisis, and publicly shied away from direct criticism of the allies. Manfred Wörner was the only exception at the systemic level, as he openly challenged the allies to adopt new policies in the Balkans. He was especially direct with the

2. Robert S. Jordan with Michael W. Bloome, *Political Leadership in NATO: A Study in Multinational Diplomacy* (Boulder, CO: Westview Press, 1979).

Clinton administration, which he felt needed to assert a more aggressive leadership role in Brussels. Wörner independently sought to implement a new security agenda for the alliance.

Certainly, Wörner's calls for change may have had a cumulative political effect on NATO, since the alliance eventually adopted the military action he desired. Yet it is difficult to draw a direct correlation between Wörner's policy activism and the eventual Operation Deliberate Force. The massacre in Srebrenica, the extensive international media coverage that came after these atrocities, and the changes in American and French foreign policy in the summer of 1995 were likely the critical factors in explaining the policy shift witnessed in Brussels. Although Wörner leaves a commendable moral legacy, his pleas in 1993 for substantial policy change had limited immediate effect on the systemic political conditions and NATO's role in the conflict.

Lord George Robertson's leadership role on the Article 4 crisis is also a good demonstration of the political limitations on the secretary general. Although Robertson was ostensibly sympathetic to the Bush administration's policy preferences toward Iraq, he still waited for a direct request from the United States before he began to actively lobby for NATO engagement and defensive measures for Turkey. Had Robertson attempted to insert NATO into the debate over Iraq prior to the Americans' request, he would have generated additional transatlantic political differences. Yet even when the American proposal came to fruition in January 2003, the wider transatlantic discord at the systemic level made diplomatic negotiations and Robertson's ability to shape NATO's agenda especially difficult. Thus, the evidence in all four chapters suggests that a secretary general can do little to shape the systemic environment, and needs American support, coupled with some backing from NATO's major European powers, before he can make a significant impact on transatlantic unity. Once some degree of consensus is reached, the secretary general can play a more instrumental role in shaping policies at the organizational level as leader of the North Atlantic Council.

LEADERSHIP AT THE ORGANIZATIONAL LEVEL

In contrast to the limited influence the secretaries general exercised at the systemic level, the North Atlantic Council (NAC) proved to be the central leadership forum for NATO's political leader, although wide variation existed in how leadership was exercised within the NAC.

The secretaries general brought different personalities and diplomatic styles to the council when interacting with NATO's ambassadors. Lord Robertson used humor to break tense moments in the alliance, but on occasion he was confrontational and tenacious in his interactions with the ambassadors. In contrast, Javier Solana rarely confronted the ambassadors and often allowed for ambiguous and free-flowing discussions. Willy Claes exercised greater control and brought more organization to NAC sessions, but, like Robertson, he would also occasionally challenge, if not "vent on," ambassadors when calling for policy change or a decision. Manfred Wörner would also directly confront ambassadors when he desired policy change, but only rarely would he become emotional in the council regarding his preferred policy outcomes.

Among the events examined in this book, Wörner's presence at the NAC meeting on April 22, 1994, is the most memorable and surely the most dramatic demonstration of the secretary general's potential influence. Multiple decision makers at that meeting maintain that his presence was vital in promoting policy consensus for military action in Bosnia. He is personally credited with affecting the alliance debate. Javier Solana's leadership role in identifying a "sufficient legal basis" for military action against Slobodan Milosevic in 1998 absent United Nations approval, and his role within the NAC in approving Option III targets to be hit in Yugoslavia, are other leadership examples that show the secretary general's power to promote consensus within the NAC. As demonstrated in Chapter 5, Lord Robertson set the NAC's agenda during the Article 4 crisis by using the silence procedure, by granting his personal support for Article 4, and through his decision to employ the Defense Planning Committee. Willy Claes also found ways, through his discretionary authority, to help promote NAC consensus for military action in Bosnia. His persistence in keeping meetings in session until consensus was achieved is another important facet of his leadership legacy.

Thus, although the position of secretary general has limited formal authority in the alliance, each leader used different diplomatic and management approaches in promoting consensus. Through a number of examples, the preceding chapters demonstrate that the NAC is a forum wherein the secretary general makes a real difference in how the alliance proceeds and, at times, is critical in influencing whether or not consensus can be reached. While this study focused only on NATO military actions, it is clear that the secretary general was often instrumental in these decisions and thus played an important role in NATO's post–Cold War evolution.

LEADERSHIP AND THE SACEUR

The third leadership forum, the secretary general's relationship with the SACEUR, provides additional insight into political leadership at NATO. All four chapters identify close partnerships between NATO's top military and political leaders, which occasionally resulted in new policy directions. In most cases, the secretaries general granted the SACEURs considerable discretion in planning and conducting military operations for the alliance. Manfred Wörner, Willy Claes, and George Robertson all generally deferred to the SACEUR on "military" decisions for NATO. Though they practiced deference, however, they did not simply allow the SACEURs freedom and independence to implement NATO's decisions without political input from them. Manfred Wörner, especially, was in constant communication with General George Joulwan as NATO policed the no-fly zones over Bosnia and as NATO ground commanders worked with the United Nations Protection Force to protect Bosnian civilians. Wörner would clearly express his frustration with the military implementation of the UN-NATO agreements, although both Joulwan and Wörner were dissatisfied with the United Nations military role in Bosnia.

In Operations Deliberate Force and Allied Force, however, the interplay between the secretary general and the SACEUR provides much insight into the actual operational conduct of these military strikes. In Deliberate Force, Willy Claes's decision to support Joulwan's request to use Tomahawk missiles, without notifying the NAC, appears to have had a significant military impact on the war which contributed to its conclusion only four days later. Claes's support for the use of the Tomahawk missiles may have been the most important military decision made during the military campaign.

During the seventy-eight-day Allied Force campaign, Javier Solana also played a key role in communicating member states' target ing preferences to General Wesley Clark. In addition, Solana was an effective diplomat for Clark during the strikes when Clark faced criticism from the allies in Brussels, or when Clark needed honest advice on politically acceptable military maneuvers. In these cases, the interplay between these NATO political and military leaders was a critical factor in the eventual success of the military campaigns.

The cases examined in this book are not alike and thus make for imperfect comparisons. The post–Cold War secretaries general led during different military conditions and political circumstances. Wörner oversaw the alliance when NATO conducted smaller, surgical strikes in Bosnia. Claes served when the alliance authorized and implemented its first sustained bombing campaign in 1995, which lasted approximately two weeks. Solana, who nearly twenty years before had opposed Spain's membership in NATO, oversaw the seventy-eight-day bombing campaign of Kosovo and Yugoslavia in 1999. The analysis of Lord Robertson's role during the Article 4 crisis differs from those in the preceding chapters because of the absence of military combat. Yet all chapters, albeit in differing degrees, focus on occasions when the alliance faced political crises that threatened its credibility. Moreover, in all cases examined, NATO successfully achieved consensus and authorized military and/or defensive measures. In such instances, it might be expected that a secretary general would play an instrumental role in shaping alliance policies. Yet nearly all preceding research on NATO's transformation devotes little analysis to the secretary general, or implicitly relegates NATO's political leader to a marginal, if not inferior, position in NATO's post–Cold War military operations. This book instead demonstrates the diplomatic, political, and military significance of the secretaries general during these decision-making processes for the alliance.

It may also be maintained that these cases are aberrant examples of the leadership of the secretaries general, examples that are otherwise not reflective of the normally limited influence of the secretary general at NATO. While these cases are admittedly not perfectly analogous, the common theme across each chapter is the identification of the secretary general's political significance, regardless of the military action contemplated. Moreover, with the exception of Willy Claes, all the post–Cold War secretaries general studied here had already had an impact on other major decisions facing the alliance prior to the actual military decisions examined. Whether it was Wörner's role in helping the alliance to accept its new Strategic Concept, Solana's role at the Madrid Summit in 1997, or Robertson's role on the Article 5 invocation after September 11, their influence appears to extend beyond these specific case studies of transatlantic crises and military action. In sum, NATO's transformation stems from many factors. Its evolution, however, must be understood, in part, from the perspective of the instrumental roles played by the individual leaders who served as secretary general.

POLICY IMPLICATIONS

These findings have some policy relevance for the alliance, especially at a time when so many observers find reasons to question NATO's future. Among this literature, many observers note the growing divide between NATO's major powers, much of which stems from the United States' and the United Kingdom's willingness to use force in Iraq absent specific approval from the United Nations.[3]

In one respect, a case can be made that NATO's current "crisis" has been exaggerated. Even with only a casual glance at the Cold War research on NATO, it is easy to identify past literature that suggested NATO's transatlantic consensus was on politically precarious grounds, but continued to survive.[4] In addition, others have noted a variety of policy areas, including its successes in improving civil-military relations in Europe's new democracies, its peacekeeping

3. David P. Calleo, "The Broken West," *Survival* 46, no. 3 (2004): 29–38; Steven E. Meyer, "Carcass of Dead Policies: The Irrelevance of NATO," *Parameters* 33 no. 4 (2003–2004): 83–97; Jolyon Howorth, "France, Britain and the Euro-Atlantic Crisis," *Survival* 45, no. 4 (2003–2004): 173–92; Ivo H. Daalder, "The End of Atlanticism," *Survival* 45, no. 2 (2003): 147–66.

4. Lawrence S. Kaplan, *NATO Divided, NATO United* (Westport, CT: Praeger, 2004); Elizabeth D. Sherwood, *Allies in Crisis* (New Haven, CT: Yale University Press, 1990); Josef Joffe, "The Enduring Dilemmas of the Atlantic Alliance," in *NATO at Forty*, ed. James R. Golden, Daniel J. Kaufman, Asa A. Clark IV, and David H. Petraeus (Boulder, CO: Westview Press, 1989); David N. Schwartz, *NATO's Nuclear Dilemmas* (Washington, DC: Brookings Institution Press, 1983), Lawrence Freedman, ed., *The Troubled Alliance: Atlantic Relations in the 1980s* (London: Heinemann, 1983); Karl H. Cerny and Henry W. Briefs, eds., *NATO in a Quest of Cohesion* (New York: Frederick A. Praeger, 1965).

and peace-enforcement successes in the Balkans, and its improved relations with Russia, where the alliance appears to have had considerable success.[5] With legitimate justification, it can be maintained that some of NATO's current skeptics neglect important areas of agreement and positive policy developments in Brussels.

At the same time, American-European differences over Iraq were contentious, and in many respects remain an ugly stain that continues to shape transatlantic diplomacy. The American deployment of thousands of soldiers to Iraq, where they face an ongoing and politically challenging insurgency, will also limit American military options in the future, and consequently will limit what NATO is capable of attempting. In addition, the political dissatisfaction over Operation Allied Force and joint military planning will certainly limit the United States' interest in future NATO combat operations, at least in the short term. Moreover, the relatively low defense-spending levels witnessed in Europe, even after the promises made at NATO's 2002 Prague Summit, arguably limit the kinds of military assistance that Europe can provide in future NATO operations.

At the systemic level, there may be little a secretary general can do except to continue to stress common security linkages and shared interests among the allies. In the Cold War, Secretary General Paul-Henri Spaak faced tremendous opposition when he sought a role as an independent policy entrepreneur, and he failed in his efforts to change NATO. Indeed, much of Manfred Wörner's legacy stems from his expressed moral conviction that NATO should be engaged in Bosnia, but even he was unable to push NATO to engage in sustained military action against the Bosnian Serbs.

Yet as was demonstrated in the preceding chapters, a post–Cold War secretary general still has greater leadership opportunities than his Cold War predecessors to shape policy—in an era when NATO's mission is much broader. NATO has demonstrated that it can go out of area and that it can conduct vastly different types of security operations.

5. Timothy Edmunds, "NATO and Its New Members," *Survival* 45, no. 3 (2003): 145–66; Joseph S. Nye, "NATO Remains Necessary," *International Herald Tribune*, May 16, 2002, 6; Harvey Waterman, "Correspondence: NATO and Democracy,'" *International Security* 26, no. 3 (2001/2002): 221–27; Dessie Zagorcheva, "Correspondence: NATO and 'Democracy,'" *International Security* 26, no. 3 (2001/2002): 227–30.

With some degree of consensus at the systemic level, a secretary general can exercise instrumental leadership within the NAC and through his relations with the SACEUR. NATO also now has twenty-six member countries, which is more than double the original twelve members in 1949. Thus, at a time when membership is so much larger, there is ostensibly a need and considerably more room for the secretary general to consult widely and promote transatlantic consensus.

The preceding chapters also demonstrate that different personalities and diplomatic styles employed by the secretaries general seem to work equally well in promoting consensus, depending upon the circumstances. Robertson's use of humor, Solana's back-room diplomacy and his sometimes laissez-faire management of the NAC, and even Claes's occasional emotional tirades were all credited as effective diplomatic tactics within their own contexts. It does seem, however, that future secretaries general should speak French. Although it is unlikely that Robertson would have been able to foster complete alliance consensus during the Article 4 crisis even had he spoken French, his French-language deficiencies certainly created additional diplomatic challenges that only exacerbated tensions within the alliance. For better or for worse, the political reality of leadership at NATO is that it requires a Francophone.

It is also important that the SACEUR and the secretary general view the alliance from similar ideological perspectives. When NATO used force in Operations Deliberate Force and Allied Force, the cooperative relationships between Claes and Joulwan, and between Solana and Clark, did much to foster transatlantic consensus and eventually resulted in successful military operations.

In a time when NATO faces critical challenges, the secretary general, then, will be an important player in shaping its future. While the secretary general's role in the alliance should not be exaggerated, and will demand American backing and some degree of transatlantic support, he can be a critical institutional player in fostering consensus. In his leadership capacity in the present age, the secretary general should emphasize the ongoing areas of consensus. Moreover, given NATO's broad and flexible strategic doctrine, the secretary general should look for new and creative security avenues in which transatlantic consensus may be identified, while also cultivating American support in the process. If the United States' preference for "coalitions of the willing" rather than NATO-supported military operations remains the norm, however, the secretary general will face tremendous political challenges in promoting consensus.

At the same time, Europe's low defense-spending levels create an ongoing security dependency upon the United States, especially should any of NATO's European allies be placed in a national security situation demanding sustained military combat abroad. Moreover, the 2005 defeat of the European Union constitutional referenda in France and the Netherlands, and the British response to postpone its own constitutional referendum, dealt a serious blow to foreign and security cooperation within the European Union—and leave NATO as the principal multilateral security organization in Europe. Within this context, NATO's secretary general has a different systemic security milieu and thus new leadership opportunities to emphasize NATO's ongoing political and military relevance.

Appendix

The North Atlantic Treaty
Washington D.C.—4 April 1949

The Parties to this Treaty reaffirm their faith in the purposes and principles of the Charter of the United Nations and their desire to live in peace with all peoples and all governments.

They are determined to safeguard the freedom, common heritage and civilisation of their peoples, founded on the principles of democracy, individual liberty and the rule of law.

They seek to promote stability and well-being in the North Atlantic area.

They are resolved to unite their efforts for collective defence and for the preservation of peace and security.

They therefore agree to this North Atlantic Treaty:

Article 1

The Parties undertake, as set forth in the Charter of the United Nations, to settle any international dispute in which they may be involved by peaceful means in such a manner that international peace and security and justice are not endangered, and to refrain in their international relations from the threat or use of force in any manner inconsistent with the purposes of the United Nations.

Article 2

The Parties will contribute toward the further development of peaceful and friendly international relations by strengthening their free institutions, by bringing about a better understanding of the principles upon which these institutions are founded, and by promoting conditions of stability and well-being. They will seek to eliminate conflict in their international economic policies and will encourage economic collaboration between any or all of them.

Article 3
In order more effectively to achieve the objectives of this Treaty, the Parties, separately and jointly, by means of continuous and effective self-help and mutual aid, will maintain and develop their individual and collective capacity to resist armed attack.

Article 4
The Parties will consult together whenever, in the opinion of any of them, the territorial integrity, political independence or security of any of the Parties is threatened.

Article 5
The Parties agree that an armed attack against one or more of them in Europe or North America shall be considered an attack against them all and consequently they agree that, if such an armed attack occurs, each of them, in exercise of the right of individual or collective self-defence recognised by Article 51 of the Charter of the United Nations, will assist the Party or Parties so attacked by taking forthwith, individually and in concert with the other Parties, such action as it deems necessary, including the use of armed force, to restore and maintain the security of the North Atlantic area.

Any such armed attack and all measures taken as a result thereof shall immediately be reported to the Security Council. Such measures shall be terminated when the Security Council has taken the measures necessary to restore and maintain international peace and security.

Article 6[1]
For the purpose of Article 5, an armed attack on one or more of the Parties is deemed to include an armed attack:

1. The definition of the territories to which Article 5 applies was revised by Article 2 of the Protocol to the North Atlantic Treaty on the accession of Greece and Turkey signed on 22 October 1951. [Note appears in treaty.]

- on the territory of any of the Parties in Europe or North America, on the Algerian Departments of France[2], on the territory of or on the Islands under the jurisdiction of any of the Parties in the North Atlantic area north of the Tropic of Cancer;
- on the forces, vessels, or aircraft of any of the Parties, when in or over these territories or any other area in Europe in which occupation forces of any of the Parties were stationed on the date when the Treaty entered into force or the Mediterranean Sea or the North Atlantic area north of the Tropic of Cancer.

Article 7
This Treaty does not affect, and shall not be interpreted as affecting in any way the rights and obligations under the Charter of the Parties which are members of the United Nations, or the primary responsibility of the Security Council for the maintenance of international peace and security.

Article 8
Each Party declares that none of the international engagements now in force between it and any other of the Parties or any third State is in conflict with the provisions of this Treaty, and undertakes not to enter into any international engagement in conflict with this Treaty.

Article 9
The Parties hereby establish a Council, on which each of them shall be represented, to consider matters concerning the implementation of this Treaty. The Council shall be so organised as to be able to meet promptly at any time. The Council shall set up such subsidiary bodies as may be necessary; in particular it shall establish immediately a defence committee which shall recommend measures for the implementation of Articles 3 and 5.

2. On January 16, 1963, the North Atlantic Council noted that insofar as the former Algerian Departments of France were concerned, the relevant clauses of this Treaty had become inapplicable as from July 3, 1962. [Note appears in treaty.]

Article 10

The Parties may, by unanimous agreement, invite any other European State in a position to further the principles of this Treaty and to contribute to the security of the North Atlantic area to accede to this Treaty. Any State so invited may become a Party to the Treaty by depositing its instrument of accession with the Government of the United States of America. The Government of the United States of America will inform each of the Parties of the deposit of each such instrument of accession.

Article 11

This Treaty shall be ratified and its provisions carried out by the Parties in accordance with their respective constitutional processes. The instruments of ratification shall be deposited as soon as possible with the Government of the United States of America, which will notify all the other signatories of each deposit. The Treaty shall enter into force between the States which have ratified it as soon as the ratifications of the majority of the signatories, including the ratifications of Belgium, Canada, France, Luxembourg, the Netherlands, the United Kingdom and the United States, have been deposited and shall come into effect with respect to other States on the date of the deposit of their ratifications.[3]

Article 12

After the Treaty has been in force for ten years, or at any time thereafter, the Parties shall, if any of them so requests, consult together for the purpose of reviewing the Treaty, having regard for the factors then affecting peace and security in the North Atlantic area, including the development of universal as well as regional arrangements under the Charter of the United Nations for the maintenance of international peace and security.

Article 13

After the Treaty has been in force for twenty years, any Party may cease to be a Party one year after its notice of denunciation has been given to the Government of the United States of America, which

3. The Treaty came into force on 24 August 1949, after the deposition of the ratifications of all signatory states. [Note appears in treaty.]

will inform the Governments of the other Parties of the deposit of each notice of denunciation.

Article 14
This Treaty, of which the English and French texts are equally authentic, shall be deposited in the archives of the Government of the United States of America. Duly certified copies will be transmitted by that Government to the Governments of other signatories.

Bibliographic Essay

Since its creation in 1949, NATO has been examined and written about from many perspectives. Within this literature, however, very little attention is devoted to the role of NATO's secretary general in shaping alliance politics. Not even editor Gustav Schmidt's three-volume tome *A History of NATO: The First Fifty Years* (New York: Palgrave, 2001) devotes any analysis to the place of secretaries general in NATO's first five decades. The one exception and seminal work on this topic is *Political Leadership in NATO: A Study in Multinational Diplomacy*, by Robert S. Jordan with Michael W. Bloome (Boulder, CO: Westview Press, 1979). Jordan's study of Lord Ismay's first organizational efforts at NATO in *The NATO International Staff/Secretariat 1952–1957* (London: Oxford University Press, 1967) also has no comparitive analysis of the personalities who shaped NATO's infrastructural development. Jordan has also written or edited the seminal works on NATO's supreme allied commander, Europe, including his *Norstad: Cold War NATO Supreme Allied Commander* (New York: St. Martin's Press, 2000) and his edited *Generals in International Politics* (Lexington: University Press of Kentucky, 1987).

Among NATO's Cold War historians, Lawrence S. Kaplan is truly exceptional. His books include *NATO Divided, NATO United: The Evolution of an Alliance* (Westport, CT: Praeger, 2004), *NATO and the United States: The Enduring Alliance* (Boston: Twayne, 1988), *The United States and NATO: The Formative Years* (Lexington: University Press of

Kentucky, 1984), his edited *American Historians and the Atlantic Alliance* (Kent, OH: Kent State University Press, 1991), and his edited book with Robert W. Clawson, *NATO after Thirty Years* (Wilmington, DE: Scholarly Resources, 1981).

Others who have written on NATO's Cold War organizational development, many of whom note the limited role of NATO's secretary general during the Cold War, are Sean Kay, *NATO and the Future of European Security* (Lanham, MD: Rowman and Littlefield, 1998); Douglas Stuart and William Tow, *The Limits of Alliance: NATO Out-of-Area Problems since 1949* (Baltimore: Johns Hopkins University Press, 1990); Dan Smith, *Pressure: How America Runs NATO* (London: Bloomsbury, 1989); Hans Mouritzen, *The International Civil Service: A Study of Bureaucracy: International Organizations* (Aldeshot, England: Dartmouth Publishing Co., 1990); Robert Hunter, *Security in Europe* (Bloomington: Indiana University Press, 1972), 61; Francis A. Beer, *Integration and Disintegration in NATO* (Columbus: Ohio State University Press, 1969); John W. Holmes, "Fearful Symmetry: The Dilemmas of Consultation and Coordination in the North Atlantic Treaty Organization," *International Organization* 22, no. 4 (1968): 821–40; Robert E. Osgood, *Alliances and American Foreign Policy* (Baltimore: Johns Hopkins University Press, 1968); William T. R. Fox and Annette B. Fox, *NATO and the Range of American Choice* (New York: Columbia University Press, 1967), 59; M. Margaret Ball, *NATO and the European Union Movement* (London: Stevens and Sons, 1959); and Ruth C. Lawson, "Concerting Policies in the North Atlantic Community," *International Organization* 12, vol. 2 (1958): 163–79.

Additional studies of Cold War issues at NATO that were useful in this research include Mark Smith, *NATO Enlargement during the Cold War: Strategy and System in the Western Alliance* (New York: Palgrave, 2000); and Michael M. Harrison, *The Reluctant Ally: France and Atlantic Security* (Baltimore: Johns Hopkins University Press, 1981).

The memoirs of NATO ambassadors were very helpful as some ambassadors were surprisingly blunt at times in their assessments of NATO and of the secretary general. *On Six Continents: A Life in Canada's Foreign Service* (Toronto: McClelland and Stewart, 2004), by former Canadian Ambassador to NATO James K. Bartleman, provides much insight into NATO's organizational culture during the

Cold War. David M. Abshire in *Preventing World War III* (New York: Harper and Row, 1988) and Harlan Cleveland in *NATO: The Transatlantic Bargain* (New York: Harper and Row, 1970) provide good, albeit limited, descriptions of NATO's secretary general during their tenures. Leif Mevik's *Det nye NATO: en personlig beretning* [New NATO: A Personal Narrative] (Bergen: Eide, 1999) was also valuable in that Mevik gives his thoughts on Willy Claes's leadership.

Given the major changes implemented at NATO after the Soviet Union's collapse, much scholarship has been devoted to the alliance's post–Cold War evolution. Among these works are Stanley R. Sloan, *NATO, the European Union, and the Atlantic Community: The Transatlantic Bargain Reconsidered* (Lanham, MD: Rowman and Littlefield, 2003); Rebecca R. Moore, "NATO's Mission for a New Millennium: A Value-Based Approach to Building Security," *Contemporary Security Policy* 23, no. 1 (2002): 1–34; S. Victor Papacosma, Sean Kay, and Mark R. Rubin, eds., *NATO after Fifty Years* (Wilmington, DE: Scholarly Resources, 2001); Celleste A. Wallander, "Institutional Assets and Adaptability: NATO after the Cold War," *International Organization* 54, no. 4 (2000): 705–35; David S. Yost, *NATO Transformed: The Alliance's New Roles in International Security* (Washington, DC: United States Institute of Peace Press, 1998); Phillip H. Gordon, ed., *NATO's Transformation: The Changing Shape of the Alliance* (Lanham, MD: Rowman and Littlefield, 1997); Robert B. McCalla, "NATO's Persistence after the Cold War," *International Organization* 50, no. 3 (1996): 445–75; and John S. Duffield, "NATO's Functions after the Cold War," *Political Science Quarterly* 109, no. 5 (1994): 763–87.

One aspect of NATO's post–Cold War transformation that has been widely examined is its expansion. See Jeffrey Simon, *Hungary and NATO: Problems in Civil-Military Relations* (Lanham, MD: Rowman and Littlefield, 2003); Jeffrey Simon, *NATO and the Czech and Slovak Republics: A Comparative Study in Civil-Military Relations* (Lanham, MD: Rowman and Littlefield, 2003); and Timothy Edmunds, "NATO and Its New Members," *Survival* 45, no. 3 (2003): 145–66. Ronald D. Asmus's *Opening NATO's Door: How the Alliance Remade Itself for a New Era* (New York: Columbia University Press, 2002) is outstanding in its coverage of the political events leading to the Madrid Summit, the summit itself, and Javier Solana's role in shaping its outcome. See also Phillip H. Gordon and James B.

Steinberg, *NATO Enlargement: Moving Forward* (Washington, DC: Brookings Institution Press, 2001); James M. Goldgeier, *Not Whether but When: The U.S. Decision to Enlarge NATO* (Washington, DC: Brookings Institution Press, 1999); and David G. Haglund, ed., *Will NATO Go East?* (Kingston, Ontario: Centre for International Relations, 1996).

Many analysts raise policy criticisms over NATO's two rounds of enlargement, including Zoltan Barany, *The Future of NATO Expansion* (London: Cambridge University Press, 2003); Tomas Valasek and Theresa Hitchens, eds., *Growing Pains: The Debate on the Next Round of NATO Enlargement* (Washington, DC: Center for Defense Information, 2002); and Thomas S. Szayna, *NATO Enlargement, 2000–2015* (Washington, DC: RAND, 2000). Perhaps the most widely cited critic of NATO expansion is Dan Reiter, "Why NATO Enlargement Does Not Spread Democracy," *International Security* 25 (Spring 2001): 41–67.

NATO's air strikes in Bosnia and Kosovo have also drawn much academic scrutiny, although much less has been written on NATO military operations conducted during Lord Robertson's tenure as secretary general. Most of the substantive research for this book relies upon openly cited or background interviews with NATO officials, as well as a wide variety of journalistic sources, official NATO documents, and speeches made by the secretaries general. Much secondary research, however, proved useful in gathering additional data for the four case studies.

On Kosovo, General Wesley K. Clark, *Waging Modern War* (New York: Public Affairs, 2001), offers a rather candid appraisal of politics within the alliance during Operation Allied Force. Benjamin Lambeth, *NATO's Air War for Kosovo: A Strategic and Operational Assessment* (Washington, DC: RAND, 2001); John E. Peters, Stuart Johnson, Nora Bensahel, Timothy Liston, and Traci Williams, *European Contributions to Operation Allied Force* (Washington, DC: RAND, 2001); Anthony S. Cordesman, *Lessons and Non-lessons of the Air and Missile Campaign in Kosovo* (Westport, CT: Praeger, 2001); and David S. Yost, "The NATO Capabilities Gap and the European Union," *Survival* 42, no. 4 (2000–2001): 97–128, are all impressive in their coverage of military aspects of the air strikes in 1999. John Norris, *Collision Course: NATO, Russia, and Kosovo* (Westport, CT: Praeger, 2005); Ivo H. Daalder and Michael E. O'Hanlon, *Winning*

Ugly: NATO's War to Save Kosovo (Washington, DC: Brookings Institution Press, 2000); Pierre Martin and Mark R. Brawley, eds., *Alliance Politics, Kosovo, and NATO's War: Allied Force or Forced Allies?* (New York: Palgrave, 2000); and Eric Moskowitz and Jeffrey S. Lantis, "The War in Kosovo: Coercive Diplomacy," in *Contemporary Cases in U.S. Foreign Policy: From Terrorism to Trade*, ed. Ralph G. Carter (Washington, DC: Congressional Quarterly Press, 2001), 59–83, also provide useful studies of the diplomacy and politics of this operation.

On NATO's strikes in Bosnia, Col. Robert C. Owen, ed., *Deliberate Force: A Case Study in Effective Air Campaigning* (Maxwell Air Force Base, AL: Air University Press, 2000), provides the most complete examination of military aspects of the operation. Mark A. Bucknam's "The Influence of UN and NATO Theater-Level Commanders on the Use of Airpower over Bosnia during Deny Flight: 1993–1995" (Ph.D. diss., King's College, 1999) is also very thorough and insightful on the interplay between UN and NATO ground commanders in Bosnia.

Other useful research on Bosnia and the diplomacy that shaped Operation Allied Force can be found in Sonia Lucarelli, *Europe and the Breakup of Yugoslavia: A Political Failure in Search of a Scholarly Explanation* (The Hague: Kluwer Law International, 2000); Tim Ripley, *Operation Deliberate Force: The UN and NATO Campaign in Bosnia, 1995* (Lancaster, UK: CDISS, 1999); James Gow, *Triumph of the Lack of Will: International Diplomacy and the Yugoslav War* (New York: Columbia University Press, 1997); and David Rohde, *Endgame* (New York: Farrar, Straus and Giroux, 1997).

Other analyses of American foreign policy toward Bosnia during the Clinton administration include Douglas C. Foyle, "Public Opinion and Bosnia: Anticipating Disaster," in *Contemporary Cases in U.S. Foreign Policy*, ed. Ralph G. Carter (Washington, DC: Congressional Quarterly Press, 2002), 32–58; David Halberstam, *War in a Time of Peace: Bush, Clinton and the Generals* (New York: Scribner, 2001); Ivo H. Daalder, *Getting to Dayton: The Making of America's Bosnia Policy* (Washington, DC: Brookings Institution Press, 2000); and Richard Holbrooke, *To End a War* (New York: Random House, 1998).

Since Operation Iraqi Freedom and the difficulties experienced over Turkey's invocation of Article 4 at NATO, much of what has been written on NATO emphasizes the political differences between the United States and Europe. Some of this research calls for NATO's reform, while some seeks its disbandment. See Sean Kay, "What Went Wrong with NATO," *Cambridge Review of International Affairs* 18, no. 1 (2005): 69–83; David P. Calleo, "The Broken West," *Survival* 46, no. 3 (2004): 29–38; Steven E. Meyer, "Carcass of Dead Policies: The Irrelevance of NATO," *Parameters* 33, no. 4 (2003–2004): 83–97; Jolyon Howorth, "France, Britain and the Euro-Atlantic Crisis," *Survival* 45, no. 4 (2003–2004): 173–92; Sean Kay, "Putting NATO Back Together Again," *Current History* 102 (March 2003): 106–12; Ivo H. Daalder, "The End of Atlanticism," *Survival* 45, no. 2 (2003): 147–66; and Robert Kagan, *Of Paradise and Power: America and Europe in the New World Order* (New York: Alfred A. Knopf, 2003).

Finally, on the research methods employed in this book, three sources were especially useful. Michael G. Schechter's article "Leadership in International Organizations: Systemic, Organizational and Personality Factors," *Review of International Studies* 13, no. 3 (1987): 197–220, provides a useful analytical framework for examining NATO's secretaries general. Robert Yin, *Case Study Research: Design and Methods*, 2nd ed. (Thousand Oaks, CA: Sage Publications, 1994), and Alexander L. George, "Case Studies and Theory Development: The Method of Structured, Focused Comparison," in *Diplomacy: New Approaches in History, Theory, and Policy*, ed. Paul Gordon Lauren (New York: Free Press, 1979), 43–68, also are instructive on case study research design.

Index

165

About the Author

Ryan C. Hendrickson is Associate Professor of Political Science at Eastern Illinois University and author of *The Clinton Wars: The Constitution, Congress, and War Powers*. He lives in Champaign, Illinois.